D0913302

*A tear-stained
journey from a life
of affluence
to one of
enduring wealth.*

Vision Publishers
PO Box 190
Harrisonburg, VA 22803
www.vision-publishers.com
ph. - 877.488.0901 • fax - 540.437.1969
email - cs@vision-publishers.com
We Welcome Your Response!

M O L L I E   B.   Z O O K

Christian Light Publications, Inc.
Harrisonburg, Virginia 22802

FROM WEALTH TO FAITH

Christian Light Publications, Inc., Harrisonburg, Virginia 22802
© 1986 by Christian Light Publications, Inc.
Printed in the United States of America

Fifth Printing, 2008

Cover design: David W. Miller

ISBN 978-0-87813-526-4

CONTENTS

INTRODUCTION

My contact with the Reimers began through our daughter and her husband (Mary Jane and Eli Miller) who served in the work at Friedensheim in West Berlin. They had met the Reimers at a youth retreat where they both served as youth counselors, and they soon came to appreciate the Reimers' staunch faith.

I first visited Hans and Netta Reimer in their own home in West Germany. They lived in a small but comfortable third-story apartment overlooking a neat little town on the Lippe River. They invited us to stay for the noon meal. Netta busied herself in her small pantry kitchen while Hans entertained us in the parlor-dining area. His quick movements and alert blue eyes indicated a man keenly aware of his surroundings.

When our daughter and her husband returned to the United States, the Reimers came with them to visit some relatives they had learned were still living in Canada and in California. We had the pleasure of having Hans and Netta in our home. It was then that we learned the touching story of their past. Often the tears came to their eyes as they related their trials and reminisced about times gone by.

But we soon learned that Hans's greatest joy came from discussing the Bible and the truths so precious to him. He carried a small Bible in his pocket, and when he spoke from it, his reverence for God's Word was clear.

Hans stated that America is in many ways ripe for the same things they experienced in Russia. But I'll tell you no more, for that is indeed the worth of this story. To Hans and Netta we owe our gratitude for this account of a journey — a tear-stained journey from wealth to faith.

—Mollie B. Zook

Chapter 1

PROSPERITY

"Elly, Elly!" Hans called from the lawn. "Ell-ee-e!" he called louder, impatiently.

Elly came running. "Here," she called cheerfully from the door.

"Papa is riding out to the farms. He says we may ride along." Hans waved his arms toward the stable where Hosi the stable boy was leading Bou, Hans's saddled pony, to the water trough.

Elly smiled at Hans's excitement as he danced from one foot to the other, still waving his arms.

"Not today, Hans. Did you forget we are having our Bible study hour here tonight? Mumsy wants me to gather some flowers for the vases."

"Ach, flowers are stupid, Elly. Come on," Hans fussed disgustedly. "Cousin Wilhelm is riding with us, and we will have a dilly with the Ulrich children while Papa tends to business."

1

Elly longed to go. There was so much to see on the farms. The air would be filled with the sweet aroma of drying hay instead of the dusty stuffiness of the village.

Elly also loved to take part in the frolics they had in the hayfields and the rides on the hay wagons. Perhaps Mattie Ulrich would let her bunch hay again with a long-handled fork. There would be cool mint tea, and . . .

"Are you coming?" Hans broke into Elly's musings. "Hosi is waiting to saddle Bunny for you," he shouted, mounting Bou with a bound.

"Maybe next time," Elly called wistfully, trying to be cheerful. "Please, Hans, be careful with your speech. You know Mumsy does not—"

Elly watched the slick dappled gray pony with Hans dash out the double gates and whiz past the white pickets that bordered the trim, spacious lawn of the elegant Reimer residence. Hans had not waited to listen to Elly's warning about his speech.

Elly turned to wave to Papa, who was now riding through the gates, rocking gently on the back of his gaited steed. He waved to Elly with a smile and a sweeping gesture of his hand.

How easily he rides, Elly thought. *Not like the impatient Hans.* She smiled again at the thought of him. She loved Hans and enjoyed joining his boyish romps and games in spite of his quick-flaring temper.

Elly snipped flowers from the flourishing beds, arrayed attractively among the rocks and borders on the lawn.

It will not be long until these beauties will be ruined by frost, she thought, *snipping a prized marigold. These with a bit of green fernery will make nice arrangements for the veranda. The dahlias with their pretty faces will add color to the parlor. Perhaps Lenchen can arrange these geraniums with the periwinkle. They would fit in with the ferns hanging in the dining room.*

"Please help me with the arrangements, Lenchen," Elly pleaded, setting her flower-laden basket on the marble topped table. "You are more gifted than I am to fix them nicely."

"I'm helping Mumsy knit," Lenchen answered curtly. "Can't you see?"

"But it can wait, Lenchen," put in Mumsy. "It is about time we put up our knitting for today, so why don't you two help each other fill the vases while I go and see if Oma Betz has supper going. We want to eat early tonight."

"Be sure to clean up any scraps or dirt from the flowers when you are finished. Then you could comb your hair before supper too," she added as she left the room.

"You choose the vases while I sort the flowers," Lenchen said, rising from her plush, cushioned chair reluctantly. "I wanted to finish this doily tonight to place on the stand in the hall," she grumbled in an undertone, so Mumsy would not hear.

"I'm sorry, Lenchen. Perhaps if we hurry, you could still finish it," Elly said quietly.

"No! Now that I had to put up my knitting, I don't want to start again tonight," she said saucily.

Elly chose a vase off the stand in the hallway. Then she chose several others from the glass china press. There was a great assortment of beautiful vases to choose from, for Papa, Gustav Reimer, had collected many rare vases during his travels.

Gustav Reimer was not outdone by anyone living in the village. His wealth showed from every corner of his lavishly furnished mansion—from the rich, buoyant carpet in the parlor to the heavy woven drapes hanging from the tall windows, his house contained the best to be had and was furnished with expensive, Victorianstyled mahogany furniture.

Gustav took pride in entertaining. His guests were treated to the best. He associated with those in popular society, keeping not only his homestead in first-class condition but his farm and business places too.

His wife, Selana, depended on Oma Betz, longtime maid and cook, to manage most of her duties in the home with the help of the young maid, Tina. Although Oma's health appeared to be good, her pace had become slower with age. Selana found herself looking after things more and more.

Selana knew her first duty was to her husband, whom she sometimes accompanied on his pleasure trips to please him. Also her children were her special care, to try to teach them and lead them in the paths she wanted them to go. This took effort on her part as Gustav left that to her, saying he had the business part to look after.

Selana was also an active worker in the church. The Mennonites were known for helping people in times of disaster or sickness, and Selana's knitting needles were kept busy to give aid where needed.

Her sympathy also reached out to the poor peasants, who had to work for the rich for such a meager wage that it barely kept them fed and clothed. Many suffered from needs that could well have been supplied by their bosses, had they been merciful. But instead, the rich were piling up riches upon riches.

True, Gustav Reimer was one of the more generous employers. Still, Selana helped their employees by handing over surplus food from the gardens and by clothing many with warm woolens that her knitting needles had fashioned. New mothers were especially grateful for the many warm garments they received from her generous hand for the little ones. The sick found balm and healing from her store of herbs and medicines and from the well-filled baskets of food that reached their doors.

Gustav enjoyed keeping his wife well supplied with rubles, for he knew she used them wisely and enjoyed having surplus to help the needy.

"Um-m-m, that borscht smells appetizing tonight," Selana commended, coming into the kitchen where Oma Betz had supper cooking.

"You cooked pork with the beets, did you not, Oma?" Selana asked, lifting the lid from the steaming pot.

"The salad looks nice too." Selana turned to where Tina the maid was adding the finishing touches to the salad plate. "You arranged it so nicely and colorfully. Gustav will be delighted. He not only wants his food to taste good, he also wants it to look nice."

"Did you bake the cakes, Tina?" Selana asked, touching their soft fluffiness with her fingers.

"Yes, Mumsy Selana," Tina answered, blushing at her praise.

"Um-m-m, they taste delicious," she added, as she pinched off a corner of one to taste.

"I'm glad you started supper a little early tonight, Oma Betz. We'd like to eat early, so we can be finished in good time before people arrive for our Bible hour." Selana patted Oma's rounded, stooped shoulders.

"Is the work getting to be too much for you, Oma?" Selana asked kindly. "Perhaps we should get another maid to help out."

"Now don't you worry your sweet head, Selana," Oma Betz said, grinning pleasantly. "These hands are used to work and would feel cheated if they could no longer help you."

"We could not do without you, Oma Betz," Selana assured her with another loving pat. "No one else can make a pot of borscht to suit my family like you can. You are not out of a job or a home as long as we are both living."

Gustav watched the two riders gallop on ahead. His heart warmed with the thought that before too many years passed, Hans would be old enough to take into partnership.

Gustav had set his hopes high for his oldest son. *Smart and sharp as my new fiddle,* he thought with satisfaction. *Plucky and quick too.*

Slapping his horse into a gallop he rode on, his thoughts still with his son, riding ahead of him. *Hans should be ready to understand some of the business at an early age, and with what I have to help him, he will make the grade and then some,* the doting father mused on. *For are not my farms located at the most favorable sites? Yes, Hans has an advantage over many other boys. Someday he might own it all, and even add or improve as he sees the most profitable. By the time Art is old enough, I might own another farm, or perhaps Art will fit in better with some of my other businesses.*

Gustav rode on with great satisfaction, viewing the fields of his friends and neighbors as he rode past. Most of the land was owned by the Mennonites, who had moved from Germany to Russia years ago and had turned the Ukraine Valley from an undesirable wasteland into the most progressive farmland in Russia.

Gustav had not lived then to know of the hardships and labor, nor of the persecutions and trials his forefathers experienced before arriving in this country for the sake of the religious freedom which had been promised to them. He had not seen the country before it had become the land of plenty.

Gustav drew in rein and slowed his horse to a slower gait. He watched more closely, for he was passing his own fields, which pastured his more than three hundred horses. Many of the young geldings and mares would soon be ready for sale.

Gustav beamed as he noticed their sleek, glossy coats. They were in fine shape. He could expect top prices.

Next he passed by the pastures where his cattle were grazing. Here too, the fatted calves were ready for market. He judged the field contained two hundred cattle besides the calves. The added rubles he expected to receive from these sales would add to his swelling bank account considerably. *Yes, I need to invest again,* he thought.

Satisfied that the horses and cattle were well taken care of, Gustav rode on, turning into one of his fields where hay-making was in progress. Hans and Willy were already on top of a hay wagon. Pat Ulrich, the overseer, was helping the men shape the top of a haystack. Gustav rode over to them.

"Nice hay you have there, Pat. You cut at the right time, just after the rain."

Pat stepped out and shook hands. "I don't think you will find any better, Herr Reimer," Pat said with a glowing grin at his boss's approval.

"I see that everything is in order and in good hands," Gustav said, turning his horse. "I have some business to attend to, so I will ride on. Tell the boys to ride back to the village in about another hour and not to wait for me."

Gustav urged his horse into a gallop, riding past acres of his well-kept vineyards. The grapes would soon be ready for the distillery. He had his own, which usually put out over a thousand buckets of wine per season. He might have to enlarge his distillery if his plans matured, but that would be no burden.

Gustav rode past the borders of his own acres for almost a mile. He rode until he came to an open field. Turning his horse sharply, he galloped up a rise to the far end of the field where a clump of white birch and a slender spruce rose above a strip of brush.

Gustav turned his horse about to get a good view of the fields spreading before him. For a few moments his experienced eyes scrutinized the fields and wooded areas. His thoughts raced through possible plans for improvements. He saw money in every foot of land.

There is a good location here for some peasant shacks without using valuable land, he reasoned. He would settle it tomorrow, which would bring his acres to a total of two thousand.

Though Gustav was elated over his prospective buy, his thoughts were not without some apprehension. There was much unrest brewing, and it appeared as if the government could be making some drastic changes. Still he rested in the fact that the Mennonites were usually favored. The government could not do without them. Being of the best farmers, they supplied much food for the country.

Furthermore, they had been promised freedom of religion. Oh, they had experienced some opposition from the unwise peasants before, but that usually blew over with no harm done to their village. He dismissed the thoughts.

But Gustav could not dismiss the thought of what Selana would have to say about buying more land. She thought he already had more business to look after than a professed Christian should have. She did not understand business too well but she did enjoy the rubles he handed over.

The thought that the church was usually ready to accept his money helped to still his conscience. And so,

Gustav brushed aside the negative thoughts and urged his horse to start homeward.

He settled back into his saddle. The comfortable sway of his horse's gait and the evening air stirring his short crop of graying hair made his ride relaxing and enjoyable.

Gustav watched the sun slip behind the distant mountains, leaving a brilliant crimson glow in its wake. His heart sang. Surely nothing would come to disturb such serenity and beauty.

Chapter 2

BIBLE STUDY

*E*lly was waiting for the boys' return. She joined them in their play as they romped around the yard. "Let's swing in the orchard yet before Papa comes," Elly suggested.

"Race you there," Hans hollered, taking off for the corner orchard in full speed.

Hans won, but he let Elly have the first turn on the swing, pushing her high in the air.

"High enough," Elly called. "Let Willy swing next."

Elly and Hans were nearly the same age. Elly had been adopted into the Reimer home when she was a baby. The Reimers had lost a baby, so when Elly came, it helped to fill the empty spot in their hearts.

The Reimers took her in as their own child, and none of them ever considered her otherwise. Hans and Elly, especially, were always very close.

Elly was a well-behaved child with a pleasant disposition. Selana often found her easier to manage than her own.

Gustav arrived home in time for an early supper. Handing the reins of his horse over to the care of Hosi, he greeted his wife pleasantly.

He did not tell her, however, what his mission had been, not wanting to trouble her with business when they were expecting company.

"Hans, have you learned your Bible verse for tonight?" Selana asked, lifting Matina from the high chair to her lap. "I should have called you in before supper. How about you, Wilhelm?"

"Uh-ah, maybe I can study mine with Hans. We were having such a good time playing I forgot, *Tante* Selana."

"Come, Art. I will get you and Matina ready for bed. Then maybe Papa will play with you awhile." Selana nodded toward Gustav with a smile.

A slight frown crossed Gustav's brow. He had planned to calculate some of the figures he had come up with on his business ride.

"It will not be for long, Papa," Selana said pleasantly. "Oma Betz will take over soon."

"Ach! Thirty minutes we have, Willy," Hans grumbled, looking at the clock in the hall. "I can learn my verse and get dressed in half that time. We will have time for a game yet," he added, grabbing a game from the closet.

"Mumsy always thinks boys poke," Hans continued with disgust. "Let's play a turn of fleet-ball. It will not take long to play that game."

"Maybe we should first learn our verses and get dressed. Then—"

"Don't waste our time, Willy. Here, take the red cup and ball. I will take the green," Hans said, pushing the cup into Willy's hand.

For a few minutes the boys tried to catch the opponent's ball with their cups. Back and forth the balls flew. Hans counted his scores quickly.

"Ten, ten, twenty. Ten off for a miss. Ten, ten, ten!" Hans had won.

"I won this time," Hans cried with glee. "C'mon, Willy, play hard, and win."

The boys played several more rounds, for Hans was not satisfied when Willy won. He had to try again so he would be the last winner.

The tall clock standing in the hall struck six-thirty.

Hans turned with a frightened jerk. "Oh, Willy! Hurry, Willy. If you don't know your verse, Mumsy will blame me."

The boys rushed through changing their clothes. Hans tugged at his bow tie, then pitched it back. He usually wore a neat, black bow tie with his Sunday shirts, but he could not be bothered tonight. They were only half prepared with their verses by the time they had to go down.

Elly was reciting her verse to Mumsy. How well she had learned it! A tinge of jealousy stung Hans to hear how perfectly she could recite it. He knew that Elly did not learn easier than he, but she applied herself, not waiting till the last minute.

Elly is good, Hans thought bitterly. *She does not get into fights, nor does she have to be disciplined often like I do.*

13

He turned away. It was no use. He could not be good however hard he tried. What hurt most was that it hurt Mumsy and made her sad when he was bad.

He did not have the peace that Elly did, not the kind of peace that Mumsy talked about—the peace that Jesus would give them if they obeyed.

Hans was certain Elly had that peace, but he was guilty. He had been bad and had used bad words. He would have to confess to Mumsy, for the weight of guilt was bearing down on his conscience. *Mumsy knows. She always knows,* Hans thought sadly. *But she also knows how to get rid of this bad feeling.* Mumsy was good. He loved her.

The pleasant evening was spent in singing and in reading and discussing the Scriptures. All enjoyed the worship services and fellowship they could have with each other.

No one was in a hurry to leave after the services. This was the time to catch up on news, not only from their own village, but from those nestled in the neighboring communities.

The younger ones gathered outside on the veranda, begging Gustav to play the fiddle for them while they sang. Gustav, being gifted in music, was willing to please them.

After some visiting among the ladies, goodnights were given, and Selana was alone.

She heard the music drifting in through the window and noticed that not only hymns were being played, but also popular folk songs. The merrymaking that was going with it saddened her. *And right after a worship time,* she thought.

With a heavy heart, she bowed her head in silent prayer.

What would my parents, or his, have thought of it all? she pondered. *Will we be able to stand fast to the faith if persecution comes?* Some in the meeting tonight thought it was near. Others did not think anything could disturb their peace and prosperity. Surely God in Heaven knew the hearts of man and was all-powerful. Would He not recompense for the trust man put in material things, instead of trusting in Him?

Selana's thoughts turned to the poor peasants. *They do the work that helps make the rich richer, yet they are neglected and often deprived of even basic needs.* She shook her head sadly. *No, the Lord will not leave us unpunished.*

Maria, Selana's sister-in-law, waited outside. Her husband, Petre, was still visiting with Gustav on the veranda after the group had left for home.

"Your flowers are gorgeous, Selana. May I have a slip of that deep red geranium?" Maria asked, stepping inside again.

"Certainly, Maria. That and any other you like."

The two mothers were suddenly startled by some yells and shrieks that came from the boys playing outside.

Hans, with his quick temper and action, had caused a fight, leaving Wilhelm with a bloody nose.

Hans repented in his mother's arms, her tears flowing with his.

"I am truly sorry, Mumsy," he sobbed, "but Willy did not speak nice about Oma Betz and I did not like that, and he . . ."

"That still does not give you any reason to hit Wilhelm, Hans. Never return evil for evil. The Bible says to return good for evil. Bad words which you happen to hear will not hurt you if you do not repeat them, and I heard you say some bad words again tonight.

"Hans, I have admonished you quite often. Now I must punish you to help you remember. For you must learn to control your temper or things will not turn out well with you later in life."

Hans hurt more from making Mumsy sad than from the punishment. He wanted to be good like Elly but he so often forgot. Maybe this punishment would make him remember.

Wilhelm gets into trouble too, Hans thought. *But* Tante *Maria scolds and shakes him as if she is angry. Mumsy does not get angry, but it makes her cry because she is sorry I am bad. Then when she punishes me, she forgives me and I can feel happy again.*

Hans thought he would not trade his mumsy for any other. He loved her dearly.

Out on the veranda, Gustav was telling Petre about the deal he was planning to make. "I rode out to see those five hundred acres that are up for sale and have decided it would be a profitable investment. It being so near to my own land makes it more desirable yet, and it is of the best land around. I have not told Selana. She might not be agreed, but she still leaves the decision up to me. Well, what do you think?"

"I'm not sure, Brother. Could be a good investment but it might not be wise if this collective farming comes into effect as is reported. Things look pretty shaky, and it appears as if there could be some deep trouble ahead with the changes in the government parties."

"Ha, you think Lenin will get his plans across? He's trying to work himself to the top by soliciting favor from the poor peasants, giving them hopes of becoming equal with the rich."

"Really, I don't believe he can do a thing. This is not the first time some fame-seeking fellow has caused disturbances among the peasants. They never got anywhere and left the peasants poorer than ever."

"Maybe not, Gustav. I hope you are right. But the way we hear, they have started a revolution already. It could reach us too."

"As I said, Petre, it is not the first time, and you know the government has promised us freedom of worship. The Ukraine really belongs to us Mennonites. They can't take it away, can they? I don't think they would want to. They know on which side their bread is buttered.

"Furthermore," Gustav continued, getting more sure of himself, "the government so far has appreciated the Mennonites. We help in disasters and in time of need. They appreciate our honesty in paying our taxes and all government dues. Our villages and farms are the pride of the country, if I have to say so myself."

"I realize that is all true, Gustav," Petre answered seriously. "Still, the reports we hear from the villages not too far distant give a person some concern. There seems to be no mercy or . . ."

"You can't always prove things by what you hear, Petre. You have to use some plain common sense and right thinking instead of being fearful and misgiving. At least there is no need to count your troubles before they hatch," Gustav added with a hoarse laugh, giving Petre a firm slap on the back.

"Well, I hope you are right, but I still don't feel too sure."

"Of course I'm right. That tract of land fits in nicely with mine. The grapes on it look promising too. I may have to add another unit to my distillery but that should be no problem. It will also give me more pastureland for the horses.

"By the way, I have quite a few that are ready for sale, and I would like to be at Vogelweg when they are put up for auction. Want to go along?"

"I wouldn't mind. They should bring a good price this time of the year. I like to attend just to watch the activities at the auction and keep up with the market."

A smile of satisfaction settled on Gustav's face. Certainly they would bring a good price. He knew when to sell. He had been in business before today.

Gustav went to bed with a feeling of security. Tomorrow he would make the final settlement that would add a fine tract of land to his own.

Chapter 3

PICNIC

———

Selana opened the note and read it. A smile spread over her face. "Lenchen," she called, "we are invited to a picnic. We must take the early train out of Wertheim on Saturday; that is, if the weather continues to be favorable."

"Oh, Mumsy, the weather has been just right for an outing. I must tell Elly."

"I think we will take a bean salad along for the picnic. What else could we take?"

"We could get Oma Betz to roast a ham, and maybe we could take some of that good cheese Papa brought home from Vogelweg."

Saturday proved to be perfect weather-wise. The party was being held at a park, and many of the Reimers' relatives were present, as well as many friends they had not seen for a long time. It was enjoyable for all.

At noon, when the tables were ready and laden with tempting foods and many goodies, someone announced the engagement of a cousin, Lisa Venfelt, to Kurt Wesserman. Congratulations were passed to the beaming couple.

This was an old-time custom of couples planning to marry, so that the date of the wedding and other arrangements could be planned with the relatives.

Hans and Wilhelm played with the group of children, taking part in the games until the newness wore off. Then they decided to explore the park area and wandered off by themselves.

At the far edge of the park, they found a more secluded place surrounded with shrubbery. Inside they found a sundial, which drew their interest. Besides, they found some comfortable seats and a smooth spot to play marbles.

All went smoothly until Wilhelm found a turtle under one of the shrubs and started to tease it.

Now Hans was fond of animals, and he did not like to see them hurt or abused, especially not when the animal was helpless to defend itself.

At first the teasing was fun, but when Wilhelm got a stick and hit the turtle, Hans could no longer stay quiet.

"Stop hurting the turtle, Willy. He did not do you any harm."

Wilhelm tried to pry the turtle open with the stick, for it had shut itself up as soon as it was molested.

"C'mon, open up," Wilhelm cried, giving it a sharp rap with the stick.

"I said quit it!" Hans hollered, trying to grab the stick. "It hurts the turtle."

Wilhelm jerked the stick out of Hans's hands. "Who is telling me what to do?" he hissed, striking the turtle harder than before. "Let him open up and come out."

Hans could take no more. Before Wilhelm knew what had happened, he was on his back with Hans sitting on top of him, pounding his chest. He no longer had the stick to defend himself.

"Let go!" Wilhelm shouted, trying to shake Hans off. But Hans was the stronger of the two. His quick action and the added strength when he was angry often gave him an advantage over many of his chums.

However, the boys' commotion brought the park guard to the scene. He took the two sober, dejected boys back to their parents, advising them to keep the boys under adult supervision.

Later, on the train when Selana had Hans on the seat beside her, she asked about the trouble between him and Wilhelm.

"But, Mumsy, he made the turtle bleed," Hans said tearfully. "And he . . ."

"It was not right that Wilhelm hurt the turtle, Hans. But neither was it right for you to hit him. Think of what the park guard thought of Christian people having boys your age who had to be guarded by their mamas so they would not get into mischief."

Hans was softly sobbing against Mumsy's shoulders.

"I was ashamed of your behavior, Hans," Selana said softly, pulling Hans down again beside her. "Had you just left Wilhelm to himself when he teased the turtle, he very likely would have tired of his play and let it go."

Hans nestled close to Mumsy. "I'm sorry, Mumsy. I wish I would not be naughty and make you feel sad or ashamed. Why can't I be good like Elly? I think I will, but it seems there is always something that makes me forget."

"We are not good by nature, Hans. All fail and come short of the glory of God. We must not depend on our own strength, or we fail. We must ask Jesus to help us. It is in His strength alone that we can overcome."

Hans rubbed Mumsy's arm while he listened. How comforting to have a mumsy who knew about Jesus and who tried to guide him to do right. What would he do without her?

"When things go wrong, try to take time to think, Hans," Mumsy continued. "Control your temper, for that is often what gets you into trouble. The Bible tells us that a man's temper does not do the things that please God. It also says not to give evil for evil, but good for evil. Always keep that in mind, Hans. It will help you as you go through life."

Hans sat in deep thought. If he always had Mumsy with him, he would not get into trouble, but he knew she could not always be with him when he was in school or playing with others. He wanted to have that strength of Jesus Mumsy talked about, to help him be good.

"I will try to remember, Mumsy dear. I do want to grow up to be good like you and . . . and Elly."

Hans laid his head against Selana. He smelled the faint, clean perfume of her freshly starched and ironed kerchief which she wore neatly pinned around her graying hair.

22

He watched two young ladies across the aisle of the coach who were giggling and trying to get attention from the other passengers. He was glad Mumsy was not dressed in gaudy and flashy attire. She didn't even wear lacy coverings as some of the Mennonite girls had begun to do. He thought they looked silly.

Hans pressed Mumsy's arm and whispered, "I love you, Mumsy. And I always feel bad when I hurt you as I did today."

Selana gave him a smile in return. Putting her arm around him, she whispered back, "I love you too, Hans. That is why I hurt when you are bad. The Bible says we should not let the sun go down upon our wrath. See, the sun is about to go down behind the mountains, so you should not feel angry with Willy any more but forgive him."

Chapter 4

THE REVOLUTION

----

*G*overnment pressure increased to bring about collective farming. The government would own everything, while the people who worked would receive a certain allotment. Everybody would be equal. No longer would the peasants be oppressed. All would have plenty to eat and wear. It all sounded very good and in the poor man's favor. The peasants were ready to fight for these promised liberties and privileges.

The dark clouds were hanging over the Ukraine too. The Mennonite name meant nothing. Like bloodthirsty hounds, the merciless officers began to tear families apart. Men were sent to the mines in Siberia or placed into prison to await a trial sometime in the uncertain future.

Gustav could still not believe that the whole plan would carry. Certainly a rich man could buy his freedom if everything else failed.

Yet the day came when he also was summoned to appear before the magistrate. When he tried to reason with them, they told him it was nothing serious and that he would be released as soon as things were straightened out. Several officers tried to console Selana with the same promises.

"I hope so," said Selana tearfully. "I have not been well lately, and I need to see a doctor. I would like to have Gustav with me when I go."

The officer bowed his dismissal out the door and called over his shoulder, "Don't worry. He will be back soon."

Gustav was not the only one taken. The courts and prisons were being filled with men. There was much delay, and some were transferred to another city to have their business hearing. Most of the men in Gustav's group were the wealthy ones.

At first they were fed and taken care of, but as the prisons were filled, food became scant, and they were treated more roughly.

Gustav tried to get a release on the basis of his wife's condition. He thought money might get him out, but it appeared as if there was always some delay. The promise of a release was always just around the corner.

At home, Selana worried more and more. Reports were far from consoling. Promises seemed to mean nothing.

Hans was in school. Even there they had much confusion. One of the teachers had been taken. Others lived in fear.

As Hans walked home through the village, dread and fear were written in many faces that had formerly been sunny and pleasant. His own held a sad expression. He had been in a fight with another boy, and as usual, he had won. He would need to tell Mumsy about it and make restitution. Mumsy would see to that. If only Papa were home. Then Mumsy would be happy again and feel better.

Hans's steps lagged as he walked across the yard of his home. Then he hurried in, anxious to have the ordeal over with.

Why were *Tante* Maria, and Uncle Petre there? All had sober, drawn faces. Uncle Fritz and Carola were there too. Then he saw Lenchen. Tears were streaming down her cheeks.

"Papa, is it Papa? What is wrong?"

Elly came to him. "No, Hans, it is Mumsy. She is very sick. The doctor is in to see her now."

Hans thought he would choke. *Mumsy, oh, Mumsy,* his heart cried. *I want you. Who will hear me and tell me what to do? Who will – ? Oh, Mumsy, I need you, now!* Hans wept.

The doctor came out of Mumsy's room. He talked in low tones to Petre. "A heart attack," he said, shaking his head. "There is no chance of recovery. I'd advise you to let Gustav know if possible. There won't be much time."

Petre consulted with Fritz. "We must try to send the message some way, but I'm afraid it is too late," he said sadly.

Oma Betz and Maria took charge of the sick patient. The doctor gave her a sedative and told them to keep her as comfortable and quiet as possible. "But do not ban anything she might ask for," he added.

In another hour, Maria came out of the sickroom.

"Mumsy wants all of the children in," she told them softly. "Be very quiet, but do come."

Hans stood beside her bed. She reached out her hand and touched him. "Remember to follow that which is good and shun that which is bad." Her voice was barely audible.

"Bring Art near that I may bless him," she said with effort, gasping for breath. Slowly she looked around at her family. With a faint smile on her lips, she blessed them all. "I'm going to Jesus, and I want you to come too. Do as the Bible says. If only Pap-a wa-ss . . ." With a smile and a weak gasp, Selana breathed her last.

Though they tried to dispatch the message to Gustav, he could not come in time for the funeral. When he did come, how pale and thin he looked! His haggard face was stricken with grief.

With weeping, he confessed to his brothers that he had been wrong. "Money cannot buy your freedom. If I could only see Selana long enough to tell her . . ." Dropping his head into his hands he wept loudly. No eyes were dry in the room.

When Gustav finally composed himself, he added, "I wanted to provide the children with a life of ease and luxury. Now I don't know what will become of them. The officers are out to get the rich, so they can take the farms. Oh, Hans and my little Art, how I would like to spare you what you may have to face in this life! Why did we not move out when the danger signals were so evident?"

Gustav knew he would be taken again, and he urged Lenchen, who was engaged, to marry a little earlier than was planned. It was only a quiet wedding, instead of the gay, festive type they had looked forward to.

Gustav gave Lenchen and her husband the bookstore he owned, where they could make their home. "As much as possible, take care of the others when I am taken again," he told Lenchen, giving her his few available rubles.

"I wish I could give you more," Gustav said sadly. "They will do me no good anymore. I only wish I had done more good for others with them while I had them in my control."

As was expected, Gustav was taken again. Hans buried his face into Bou's mane. Why did he have to give up all that he had? Mumsy, dear Mumsy, who had understood a boy of twelve, had taught him what was good, and had punished him when he was bad. He wanted to be good, but there was no one to confide in now. No one to wipe away his tears and give him the assurance he needed. Now they had taken Papa. Hosi had left too. Nothing was normal, and now he must part with his pony and move to town with Lenchen. She had already found a job for him at a plant, painting machinery.

The revolution spread in earnest. The rich people were taken, and the children were turned out of their homes to fare as they could. Friends or strangers took children in, sharing the little food they had. No one had enough to satisfy their hunger.

Chapter 5

DRAFTED

———

*L*enchen answered the light knock on the door. She was surprised to see Pat, the Reimers' former plantation overseer.

"Please, Lenchen, may I speak in privacy?" Pat asked, trembling visibly.

Lenchen drew him inside and motioned him to come to the back of the upper apartment. "You have news?" she questioned with her eyes.

Pat drew a deep breath. How Lenchen had aged in the eight years since the revolution began, and how thin she was. His eyes grew misty, and the lump that stuck in his throat choked him, so that he could not trust his voice to speak.

Lenchen pulled out a chair. "Do have a seat," she offered.

"You take the chair, Lenchen. I have but a moment, and I do not want to cause any suspicion of being a news carrier. Are we safe?"

Lenchen drew the curtain. "I think so," she whispered, as she dropped into the chair, trying to brace herself for the worst.

"Is it Papa?" she whispered.

"Yes. Your Uncle Frank gave me a message to deliver. He and his family are trying to leave the country. Escape! I fear they will not make it. It is very dangerous."

"Yes, I know," Lenchen said tearfully. "If only we would all have gone in time. They have taken my Fritz too," she added with a burst of tears.

"I'm sorry, Lenchen," Pat said softly. "It is a sad time. Now Frank did not see your papa, but he received some information from one who knew. Your papa was forced to stand in cold water up to his waist. They said there were a thousand men punished this way. Tortured! Many of them died. Though he had no direct word that your papa died, they feel confident he did. No one can take such exposure for long."

Lenchen's sobs were the only sounds in the room for a minute until she composed herself. "How horrible," she finally whispered. "Tell me everything," she said. "I want to know it all."

"There is no doubt that many of the men were forced to stand so long that they finally succumbed and sank into the water. But Bishop Hartmut, how terribly they tortured him," Pat continued. "It seems they have no mercy on any religious man. Frank said they took a hook and fastened it to the bishop's nose. They hung him up by his nose!"

Lenchen could only weep.

"I must be going, Lenchen. I am sorry to bring such sad news, but Frank was afraid you might never find out about your papa."

"I'm so thankful you came, Pat. Any information you can bring me concerning our relatives I'll be so glad to know. Elly is married. Hans is twenty now and will soon be drafted to serve in the army. One does not know from one day to the next what might happen. No one has enough food anymore. Sickness and death are heard of day by day. There are no doctors. They have been taken too. No more church or Bible hours. Fear and suspicion have taken over," Lenchen whispered, leading the way to the door.

"I'll let you out through the back entrance, Pat. *Gott befohlen.*"

"Keep your religion to yourself, Lenchen. They are taking women too, shipping them like cattle to Siberia."

"I know," Lenchen whispered as she let Pat out and closed the door softly. She never saw him or heard of him again.

The evening shadows lengthened, deepening the gloom that hung over the dismal homes in town. Only a few late workers walked the broken, rough streets, slowly, dejectedly homeward. The only noise was the barking of a dog, answering another's faint barks out of town. The whole town was draped in mourning, like an untimely shroud.

The playful laughter of happy children was silenced too. Instead, their large, longing eyes told of the hunger that was ever present, that could not be satisfied with their allotment of bread.

The shadows faded, and darkness hid the filthy streets and eerie alleys. No lights shone from the windows. Not a ray of light or warmth cheered the few wanderers in the streets.

The hour was getting late. Still Lenchen remained sitting with her head resting on her arms across the small table. She must think!

With most of her family gone—husband, Papa, Mama, aunts, and uncles—what was her next move?

Should she go to the Caucasus, where Aunt Freda had taken her brother Art and sister Matina? If she went and Fritz would be released, would he be able to find her? Or should she, like Uncle Frank and Gabi, try to escape to freedom? Would it be worth the risk?

Lenchen still had the rubles hidden that Papa had given her before he was taken the last time. Since she worked at the factory, she had added some to the savings. She could not use it for food, for there was none to buy. Lenchen had also earned some money by knitting at night. There would be enough to pay her train fare to the Caucasus, where the revolution had not as yet been so serious. But how long would it stay that way? Eventually, the revolution would spread all over Russia. If she would buy a ticket for Kaunas, she would be near the border. Perhaps she could escape to Germany. But reports were that the borders were closely watched.

Lenchen reasoned that since her forefathers came to this country from Germany for religious freedom, it might now be possible to return to Germany. Since they were still

Germans, perhaps there was a chance, even though now they were Russian citizens.

Hans would have to go to serve his military training, so Lenchen would not be responsible for him any longer.

Lenchen finally decided to visit Bart and Elly. Maybe they would like to escape too, if they knew that Uncle Frank had tried.

But then there was the factory to deal with. Would they grant her a few days' leave? Hans wanted to visit Elly before he left. She would try to get a pass, so they could go together.

"Do you really have to go, Hans?" Elly questioned, wiping the tears that flowed with the happy reunion of the three. "What would Mumsy say? She did not believe that anyone should fight or kill. She even thought it was wrong to enter military training."

"I hope I never need to fight, Elly, much less kill," Hans said with feeling. "They can do with me what they want, but I don't intend to fight. There is enough sorrow and suffering as it is."

"I hope you keep that conviction, Hans," Elly said soberly. "But two years, or two and a half, may bring some changes that you do not realize now."

"Oh, Hans," Lenchen gasped, shivering with fear, "I'm afraid for you. Already most of our family is gone. Mumsy is not here anymore to help us do what is right. She so often told us what the Bible said, that we should not do evil, but good. But poor Mumsy is not here to see and know what we experience now."

"That is true, Lenchen. But I know Mumsy not only believed the Bible, she lived it. She would rather have died than do what she thought was wrong. I will never forget how the night she died she asked God to take care of us."

For a few moments their tears flowed silently. How they needed her for counsel and admonishment.

"Maybe this awful revolution will be over soon. Then things might be different again," Elly said hopefully. "But I fear every evening that the Bolsheviks will come for Bart."

"It is a dark picture, Elly," Hans said sadly. "But we do hope things will be better someday."

"It is not the Russian people in general," Lenchen remarked softly. "They have befriended us in many ways. What would have become of the children when they were chased from their homes, if people had not taken them in? Heartless Bolsheviks! Nothing is too gruesome for them."

"That is true, Lenchen, but be careful about voicing your opinions. There are also many who will do them a favor for a piece of bread. If they betray you, well, off to Siberia you go."

"Let's reminisce on our good days at home yet before Hans leaves," Elly pleaded, smiling. "It is so good to think back sometimes and forget the present difficulties. Remember how Mumsy always brought sunshine into our lives?"

And so they reminisced. Though some incidents which they recalled brought smiles and laughter, their conversations would still be drawn to the present hard times. It was not easy, having been so accustomed to riches and luxury, to now live like the poor peasants or even worse.

When it was time for Hans to leave to catch the evening train, Elly clung to him. "Hans, Hans, will I ever see you again? Please write if you can."

Tears blinded Hans's eyes as he kissed Elly good-bye. "Keep the faith, Elly, as much as you know how. We will meet again," he whispered, patting her shoulder.

Hans spoke with more confidence than he felt. He would have to take six months' training, then give two years in service. With the present conditions, much could take place before he came home.

The conductor was calling, "All aboard!" Hans tore away from his sisters and ran for the train. The two girls waved as long as the train was in view. Then it rounded the bend at the edge of a forest and was gone.

Arm in arm, Lenchen and Elly retraced their steps. No words were spoken, but they wiped tears frequently. Not until they were safely inside Bart and Elly's apartment did Lenchen voice her undecided plans.

"No, Lenchen. Bart and I are still together, though he can come home only on weekends. I have work several days a week doing bookwork and that helps too. If we work faithfully, maybe he will not be taken, but if we were caught trying to escape, you can be certain we would be disposed of."

"I'm not sure what I will decide, Elly. But it seems to me nothing could be worse than to suffer persecution in Siberia or face a death like Papa or the bishop faced. It is all so frightening."

Lenchen did not press Elly. The two sisters parted, not knowing when or if they would see each other again.

Chapter 6

NETTA

---

*T*wo warmly dressed border guards were riding their horses along the border on night duty. The night was cold, and they reined in their horses behind a clump of birch that sheltered them a bit from the strong west wind.

"Ha, Dieter, it is you," Hans hailed his companion with a quick salute. "A cold night! Glad when they change shifts. Another hour to go."

"Yeh! Wrap your blanket around your ankles and feet as I do. It keeps the horse's warmth inside. Helps a little."

Hans tried his comrade's advice. It did help.

"Say," Dieter called above the shrieking wind, bringing his horse around to face Hans's steed, "have any leave coming up? Say in a month from now?"

"Hardly, Dieter. I was called into service later than you. I doubt if they will give me a leave yet."

"Perhaps I can put in a word that would give you an early leave." Dieter paused. "Uh, you see, I will be having one, and I need a best man, you know, to stand with me when I get married."

"I see. Who is the lucky girl, may I ask?"

"Carola Hackbert. She lives near your town, and maybe you could visit your kin at the same time."

"Sounds great, Dieter. You get the leave, and I will be more than willing to go." Hans, however, had his doubts. Dieter would be ready for his release in another six months, while Hans had put in little more than that. Their lieutenant commander kept them buckled down and wasn't lenient to any.

Somehow, Dieter won. Did a wedding make a difference? The lieutenant even cracked a thin, crooked smile as he handed them their passes.

Hans was introduced to the bridal party. There were two bridesmaids. One of them was introduced to him as Netta Neufelt. Hans was impressed at once. She had her white kerchief pinned neatly around her wavy blond hair just the way Mumsy used to wear hers. There was also something about her that reminded Hans of a little girl he had known when he was a small boy. He hoped to learn to know her better at a more convenient moment.

Netta sang at the wedding. Her voice was beautiful. Hans's deep bass blended well with her soprano.

Tears stung Hans's eyes at the serenity of the hymns. It was all such a contrast to the loud bugles and the blaring of the country's anthem heard daily at the camp.

True to Hans's thinking, he and Netta had known each other when they were children. Meeting at times at the park parties, they had played together in the games. He remembered her as one of the quieter, more sensible girls who would put her all into the games without being loud or boisterous.

The two struck up a friendship, and when Hans took leave to visit his sisters, she promised to correspond with him. He left with more spring in his step and more warmth in his heart than he had known since Mumsy died.

Hans found his sisters well, with the exception of stress and lack of nutrition. More and more people were being taken. They all lived in suspense and fear. Nobody trusted each other anymore.

When Hans left, the parting was sad, but Hans still had hopes that by the time he had served his two years, things might be better. Lenchen and Elly were happy that he had found a friend. They promised to look her up when they could get away.

Dieter returned from his leave a week later than Hans, and he brought a little package for Hans. It was from Netta. The package contained a few nuts and sweet cakes. A note was included.

She wrote that she was well and hoped he was too. She thanked him for the nice time they had had the day he had taken her to the park. She had enjoyed the day and was glad they could get acquainted.

Warm circles raced around Hans's heart to realize she cared. The nuts and cakes were almost too precious to eat. He had not tasted anything so delicious for a long time.

Hans tried to get another leave when Dieter was released. But this time he had no success. His time of service was nearing the end before he had another leave. In the meantime, letters needed to be short, and they were all read and examined before they were sent. It was the same way when he received any. But both Hans and Netta seemed to be able to read between the lines, and their brief acquaintance deepened. Both were anxiously waiting the day when they could see each other again. Yet the tense conditions of the country continued to concern them.

During Hans's leave before his final six months of service, he and Netta made plans for their marriage. They decided to keep it a secret until he returned to stay and then get married shortly after the engagement was announced.

The long-awaited day finally came. Hans was traveling home by rail, and Netta and her mother were making plans for a picnic for a few close friends and relatives to announce Hans and Netta's engagement. It would be far from elaborate, but nice enough to make an enjoyable day at the park with some refreshments. A dress of Mutti's was being adjusted and remade for Netta to look her best. She would likely wear it for her wedding dress too.

Many soldiers were crowded into the coach on which Hans was riding. Hans was disgusted at their drinking. It made him even more thankful that Mumsy had not let them drink strong drink, even though Papa made it. Hans had no desire to have any, though it was frequently offered to him and he was ridiculed for abstaining from it.

Hans handed his papers and pass to the officer behind the desk. All he needed was to have his release confirmed with a stamp on his pass, showing the country's approval of service rendered, and he would be on his way to see Netta. His heart warmed at the thought. Netta, his beloved!

Hans's patience was tried. Why should it take so long to get the papers in order? Were they lost? Or was the right person not in with the authority to stamp his pass?

When his name was finally called, Hans marched up to the desk, with a pleasant whistle of joy on his lips. Opening a drawer, the officer took out a stamp and stamped Hans's pass with more punch than was needed and handed it over, his face drawn into a wicked frown.

Hans started to leave, glancing at the pass with its bold stamp glaring back at him.

Hans stopped short, examining the stamp the officer had applied. He turned back to the desk. "Sir, there must be a mistake. That stamp . . . er . . . I . . ."

Pushing his bristled face close to Hans's, the officer hollered, "There is no mistake!" Turning his back on Hans, he walked into another room.

Stunned, Hans remained rooted for a moment. The stamp was a Wolf's Pass, which meant Hans was "socially strange and not to be trusted."

Hans was numb with grief. He was doomed! With such a pass, he would not be able to get a job. He could stay at no one place longer than twenty-four hours. He would be chased about like a rabbit with a hound on its tracks.

Hans walked slowly and dejectedly down the street. He would see Netta, but there would be no wedding. Like other rich men's sons, he had no chance. The government was taking no risk of the boys trying to claim their father's rights and farms which had been taken.

"Netta, oh, Netta!" Hans's heart cried. He tried to compose himself for her sake.

Chapter 7

ON THE RUN

*N*etta welcomed Hans joyfully, her eyes shining. Hans's heart skipped a beat. How he longed to tell her with confidence that he had come to claim her promise! But it could not be.

Netta was not only disappointed, but heartbroken when Hans showed her his Wolf's Pass. Her hopes and dreams for this hour were dashed. All the preparations had been made for naught. Could she live on without Hans? It seemed impossible.

For some time, cold shivers raced through her body. It seemed as if the shock had turned her heart into a cold stone for heaviness. She could not think properly. She could not even shed tears.

With effort, Netta relaxed, and the tears started to flow. Hans wept with her for a few moments.

"Netta, we must face reality," he whispered brokenly. "Let's hope this war and hatred will pass, and we can be reunited before long."

"I am sorry, Hans. It is true. We are no longer children and must face life as it is, with its disappointments and sorrows. Please forgive me for my weakness. Though we must be parted, we can still love.

"You cannot stay," Netta added, drying her tears, "or they might take you right away. They will be on the lookout, you may rest assured."

"You know, Netta, we may not even correspond. Since I must keep on the move, you will not be able to write to me. And should I write to you, it would give the authorities some evidence of where I am staying.

"Netta," Hans continued hesitantly, "we must depend on a higher power than man. I know there is a God. Mumsy taught us that. I cannot realize how a good God can let such hate and greed take over, but maybe He will end it soon. Let's pray that it may be soon."

"I . . . I don't know how, Hans," Netta whispered softly.

"Let's try to learn more about God, Netta," Hans whispered back.

Hans rose as if to leave.

"Please," Netta pleaded, "do not leave yet. It is not dark enough to make it safe. Besides, you need food to refresh yourself."

Mutti rose from her seat. "Yes, do stay for supper before you start on your way. It might be hard to find food. We will also fix some food to send with you."

Hans could not resist their offer. Netta stepped nearer. "Hans, I would like to hear your plans . . . if you have any, and if you care to share them."

Hans dropped his head into his hands for a moment. "First," he said, "I would like to see my sisters before going further. Then . . . what can I do?"

"Oh, Hans, I feel so helpless. If only I could help in some way."

"Pray, Netta. Pray. Mumsy always said that God is near and is a very present help in time of need. I wish I knew more about it."

"I will try, Hans, but I am not sure how to pray," Netta repeated, dropping her eyes in embarrassment from Hans's pleading gaze.

"I know there is not much use to make definite plans in these disturbing times, Netta dear," he whispered, "but I thought I might try to catch a freight for the Caucasus. Maybe I can find Art and Matina. They went there with my aunt, you know."

"That would be nice. I hope you find them." Netta smiled through her tears.

"Of course, it may be that I can find snatches of work here and there. I hope I can on the way down at least, for I need money to buy food."

Hans and Netta clung to the short time they had, trying to make good use of what little was left. But parting was unavoidable, and the seriousness of the situation left them in nearly wordless suspense.

Netta had braced herself for the parting, hoping to be brave for Hans's sake, but she failed utterly. With tears streaming down her face she offered him her hand.

"I will think of you often, Netta," Hans said as he took Netta's hand. "And it will strengthen me to know that you will pray," he whispered brokenly.

Netta could not speak, but she smiled and nodded.

"Please do not forget me, Netta," Hans pleaded with a last fond look into her tearful eyes. "Let us pray and hope that our parting may not be for long."

Hans waited as if to prolong this moment. Then tightening his grip on her hand, he bent closer. "I'll come again," he breathed softly. Opening the door, he slipped out into the night.

Hans walked all night, keeping off the road as much as possible and hiding in ditches or behind hedges when the light of a car came near.

Lenchen was surprised to see him at the door when she answered the knock late in the night. She sympathized with Hans. "Too bad it turned out this way," she said sadly. "We know now that we will never get any benefits from what Papa owned. Rather, his riches have become a snare for us. But we know now how some of the poor people existed then."

"Why don't you go with me to see Elly, Lenchen?"

"I believe I will, Hans. There is a late bus running in that direction, and I feel you will be safe to travel there with me."

"I'm sorry, Lenchen, but I do not have money for fare. They did not give me any at the army station when I left."

"Don't worry, Hans. I still have a few rubles here that Papa gave me, and it was given for a time like this, I'm sure."

The two reached their destination in the early morning hours. Elly was glad they had come early, for she had to work that day. The three lost no time in discussing the problems at hand. "I'm so glad that you will try to find Art and Matina, Hans, and that you are traveling to the Caucasus. For you will be safer there than in the areas farther north."

Lenchen took the early bus home while Hans slept at Elly's apartment until evening when it was more safe to travel.

Elly and Hans clung to each other in parting. Always there was a fear that they might not meet again. "I will pray, Hans—pray and pray, for God knows what is best, as Mumsy would say."

Hans was determined to see his childhood home once more. In the dark, he crossed the fields that lay behind the village and Papa's home. The moon shone brightly now, and he could easily see the outline of the buildings. Walking nearer, Hans saw that the fence was torn down, and things were not kept up. It was disgusting. *What do they want with the place if they let it fall to pieces?* Hans wondered. His bitterness increased when he thought of the home it would have made for him and Netta. Yes, he'd even be glad to have one of the peasants' houses.

A dog barked, and Hans drew back into the shadows. With one last longing look, he slipped through the bordered hedge, turning his back forever to the place he used to call home.

Hans had not waited long at the railroad until another traveler joined him. Had it not been for the looks of the stranger, Hans would have been suspicious.

"Good evening, friend," Hans greeted the stranger. "Looking for a ride?"

"You too?" the stranger asked.

"Yah," Hans grunted, looking the stranger over. His clothes were badly soiled, and his gaunt, half-starved figure told Hans all he needed to know. Opening the bag Netta and his sisters had filled, he offered the man a small hunk of bread. Hans felt certain he had not eaten for some time.

He saw the stranger wince as he accepted the handout with sincere thanks. He ate very slowly, making the food last as long as possible.

He turned to Hans again. "Thanks, buddy," he said hoarsely. "My name is Andi Klinsky. From uh . . . up north."

Hans wished he could give Andi more but knew he had to be careful to save for future needs. "I'm Hans Reimer. Did you get a special stamp too?" Hans asked, shaking hands with Andi.

"If you want to call it special, yes. I call it a curse and a ruination to mankind," Andi whispered. Even in this solitary place, no one dared to voice his opinions freely.

"To the Caucasus?" Hans asked cautiously.

"To anywhere away from these wolves who seek to tear you apart," Andi answered with disgust.

"Or starve you and chase you," Hans muttered under his breath. "Come with me. We are in the same boat. Your dad was rich too?"

Andi turned his face away and sighed deeply. "He was, but he is no more. They . . ." Andi's voice broke. "Tell me about yours."

"I have the same story to tell. Those yet living are scattered, and we can hardly expect to see them all again."

The two boys hid in the grass when they saw the lights of the oncoming freight. It being a long train, the engine passed them before coming to a complete halt. After switching some cars, the signal whistle blew, and the engine started again. The boys ran and boarded before it picked up much speed.

"We will have to leave the cars before they stop, Andi. For, once the train stops, they are likely to search for riders and turn us over to the police."

Andi appeared to be in a daze. Hans was glad he could be there to help him. He offered Andi another hunk of bread from his bag.

At first Andi refused, turning his face away. "Keep it, pal. It is yours, and you need it as well as I."

"We are in this together, Andi. Perhaps there will be some to be had when we leave this train."

Reluctantly, yet hungrily, Andi accepted. "If we cannot get work, we cannot get bread, for we have no ration cards."

"No, and I do not want to steal either, Andi. My mother was a good woman. She tried to teach us what was right. But she died when I was only twelve, and it is so hard to remember."

"My father was a preacher, Hans, so you can be sure they finished him up in a hurry too. My mom is . . ." Andi choked, clearing his throat in an effort to relate the sad story. "They took her, and no doubt she is in Siberia if she didn't die on the way. They ship them in cattle cars and pack them in worse than they would cattle. It is so cold, many never arrive alive. It would be some consolation to know that she died, rather than thinking she might be slaving in the mines. Mom was not a strong woman and never had to do hard labor."

Andi bent his head between his knees and sobbed — heartrending sobs that seldom escape the bosom of a grown man.

Hans's tears mingled with his in sympathy. "Andi, many of us know about those sorrows too. I left my dear bride-to-be behind, besides two sisters. If we get to the Caucasus, I might be able to find an aunt, my brother Art, and sister Matina."

The boys got off as soon as the train slowed enough for them to get off safely. They stayed hidden until night. "Could we venture out now?" Andi asked. "I'm so thirsty and hungry too."

"Not safe yet, Andi. Not as long as you see lights and hear dogs bark. We want to go to the depot here and see if we can find a friendly clerk or ticket agent. That would not be safe yet."

Trying to stay awake, the two waited in silence. At last they walked along the tracks and came to the large depot.

The ticket agent knew what they wanted without asking. The dirty clothes and haggard appearance always told the story of boys in desperate needs.

"Come back in here," he motioned to the boys. "Get washed. There is some bread back there too, in case you are hungry," he whispered. The station was almost deserted this time of night.

Before they were finished, the kind man came back to them. "Stick around till morning. I will find you some white aprons that will class you as help. You can carry passengers' luggage and help them to the trains.

"The pay is small—just what the people give you, but it keeps starvation from taking over," the man added. "With a white apron and a number you will be able to buy from those who have food stands in here to sell to the travelers." The ticket agent came close and whispered in their ears. "Now beat it. And beware of the police!"

When the boys came out, the station had filled considerably. It was not hard to mingle with the crowd, then venture farther away from the gates where the passengers boarded. In a corner away from the light, the two crawled under a bench, and were soon fast asleep.

However, the tension they were under woke them in good time. They received their aprons before the next train came in. It was from a large city and a big crowd piled from the coaches. Hans and Andi were not the only ones with white aprons offering help, but Hans never did find out if the others were hired under the same conditions. Such things were not discussed in public.

Hans and Andi were well pleased with the coins the passengers gave them in return for their service. Hans realized that even government men were among the passengers who paid them. Everybody seemed to be in a hurry and paid little attention to who helped as long as they wore the identifying aprons.

On the second day of their service at the depot, Hans and Andi were waiting on the platform outside. A train was just pulling in. Another was coming in the distance. The whistle and roar of the engine was drawing nearer by the moment. Here was another chance to earn a few coins, since both trains came from the big cities. But Hans's sharp ears heard another sound. He nudged Andi. "Police," he whispered, just as he saw a uniform pass one of the open gateways. "Quick," Hans whispered, slipping between two cars that were standing on the track. The first train had stopped, and the passengers were pouring from the coach near them. Instead of mingling with the stream of people, Hans and Andi went the other way, slipping between cars until they were lost to those at the station.

Running down the track, they hid behind some barrels and boxes.

"That was close, Hans. I did not hear anything out of the ordinary."

"Andi, when you are being hunted, you have to develop keen ears and eyes. If they catch us, it will be Siberia or jail."

Whenever another train hid them from view, the boys crept farther away from the station. When they were at a safe distance, they hid in the grass until nighttime. They would hitch a ride to the next city in hopes of receiving aprons again.

Hans and Andi did find other ticket agents willing to help them. They would each receive a number and a new white apron. Yet their jobs always lasted but a short time until the police searched the area. They were accustomed to being on the alert at all times. They also learned there were many sympathetic Russians. Even the poorest families helped what they could.

The boys often traveled different directions and routes, crisscrossing the country, instead of going directly to the Caucasus. But they did eventually reach their destination.

Here they found work at a large farm operated by a German organization. The organization not only rented the land, but had a construction company too. They could hire a great number of men. They had around a thousand horses and grew much grain, especially soybeans. The revolution had not yet reached them.

For more than a year, Hans took care of horses, helping Andi train them. Andi proved to be a capable horse trainer, and Hans enjoyed working with him.

"Andi, I'm afraid you are too relaxed in this place," Hans warned him. "Remember, there is no place of security for us."

The reports they received of the revolution did not appear favorable to Hans, and he was on the alert all the time.

From April of 1932 to November of 1933, the boys lived quite a normal life, but as time went on, the revolution drew closer.

"Be prepared, Andi. One of these days we will have to flee again," Hans warned. But Andi only smiled at Hans's anxiety.

"Going to help me clean the stables tonight, Andi?" Hans asked one evening.

"Sure, buddy. Not going to let you do all the work," Andi grunted, grabbing a pitchfork.

The two worked side by side in silence, pitching the manure out a window that was left for that purpose. "Give them a nice bed of straw too," Andi said, hoisting another large forkful of manure.

Hans listened. A vehicle different from those his ears were accustomed to was coming near. Poking Andi with his fork handle, Hans leaped out the window. He was not taking chances.

Hans moved not a minute too soon. But Andi, looking first to see what was going on, was caught.

Hans and another worker fled deep into the woods before they stopped to catch their breath. "Oh, Andi!" Hans panted, when he realized Andi had not followed. "Why didn't you come?"

Chapter 8

SOAKED

———

*H*ans felt a great sorrow for Andi. He had loved him like a brother.

Heinerich Stafven, the other man who had escaped, had seen the police just as they crowded the horse stable. Andi and a few others were taken.

"Where can we go?" Hans gasped as the two sat down on an old log. The overgrown vines and brush made the spot a good hiding place for the moment.

Heinerich hung his head between his knees, choking for breath. When he finally raised his head, Hans saw that his face was ashen. "My heart," he whispered.

Hans supported Heinerich's head on his lap. "Stretch out on the log until you feel better," he advised, rubbing his arms and body.

"We will rest awhile." Hans tried to sound cheerful. "They will not find us here."

The two boys rested and slept. They longed for water and food, knowing they had to move on, but not knowing how far they might have to walk before they would find anything to eat. It being November, no berries were to be found in the woods. And so they traveled west, hoping to find a village.

It was dark the second night after their escape by the time they reached a village, and Heinerich thought it looked familiar. He knew of a boarding house there.

The hostess answered their knock. She was known as Yoch's wife and remembered Heinerich's father. "Go to the back entrance," she whispered, "so as not to cause suspicion."

The two walked on, then circled through an alley. Yoch's wife met them at the back door and locked it behind them.

"I will have work for you right here," Yoch's wife answered, after hearing the boys' story. "This place needs some repair work and painting too. You will receive board for pay. And I will help keep watch for your safety."

The boys expressed their gratefulness, and Yoch's wife went to prepare for her guests for the night.

"We are very hungry!" Heinerich exclaimed at last.

"We are sorry to bother you at this time of night, but since we did not have food for some time, we would be better prepared to work in the morning if we could eat a bit before we sleep," Hans stated, yawning.

"I should have thought that much," Yoch's wife said, leaving the room. She soon returned with bread, cheese, and some goat's milk. How delicious it tasted to the hungry boys!

Giving the boys each a blanket, she showed them a closet under the stairs where they could sleep.

"Here's a bag of rags," Hans said cheerfully, pulling it out of a corner of the closet. "This will make a dandy pillow for both of us."

With their stomachs satisfied, the boys slept well and were refreshed to start a new day's work.

The boys learned that Mr. Yoch lived upstairs and took care of those apartments. They had made this arrangement to keep their identity more secret. Tension and fear seemed to be everywhere.

The boys remained at the boarding house for several months. After they had finished the work there, Yoch's wife found them some work in the village. Most of it was night work and they slept during the day. They still received their board, but earned slightly more than it took to pay for their keep.

Hans opened his sleepy eyes. Yoch's wife was calling them from outside the stair closet. "What's wrong?" he asked sleepily. "Surely not time to get up for work, is it?"

"I've brought you an early supper, boys," she said almost in a whisper.

Hans was wide awake now and was shaking Heinerich. "Wake up at once. We are in trouble," he said hoarsely.

A smile spread over Yoch's wife's face when the two frightened faces appeared from the closet. "I was in the village and met a military man. He told me to tell you boys to be at home tonight, for he had a few questions to ask. 'Nothing serious,' he said all too calmly." With a wink at the boys and another smile, she set the two bowls of soup on the floor and turned to leave.

"Wait," Hans called softly. "We want to pay what we owe. Three days, not?"

But Yoch's wife waved her hand. "Nothing," she said with feeling. "You will need that." She closed the door softly, and that was the last time they saw her. But they never forgot her kindness.

"It's not dark enough yet, Hans," Heinerich said quietly into Hans's ear when he saw Hans gather up his belongings. "They will catch us for sure."

"I know well what kind of questioning they have," Hans hissed through gritted teeth. "We must leave at once. Don't lose any time, Heinerich. We cannot stay and put Yoch's wife and the boarding house in danger." Hans spoke in earnest.

"Come, I'm going. We will hide in that haystack back there in the field. The hedge will hide us while we go," he whispered.

"Keep in the shadows as much as possible, Heinerich," Hans said, opening the door and running for the shed behind the boarding house.

Nothing more was spoken. Hans did not look to see if Heinerich was following or not. They hated to leave without saying more to Yoch's wife for her kindness, but she must not know what became of them.

Slipping out through a loose board on the back of the shed, the boys crept along the hedge, bending low. They had to cross the field when they came to the end of the hedge. Lying flat on their stomachs, they snaked slowly through the grass, reaching the haystack in safety.

"Help me dig a hole here on the woods side of the haystack," Hans ordered, crawling around the stack. "Here we can hide safely till dark, unless someone saw us come out here, and I doubt that anyone did."

Heinerich obeyed without question. He had learned that Hans seemed to sense what was best for their safety.

Inside the haystack, the boys covered with hay the hole they had dug. "I hope there are no suspicious-looking spots out there," Heinerich said, catching his breath and relaxing in the hay.

"We will be on the lookout, and it is cloudy. Rain would help us get to the woods without getting the village dogs roused. As soon as it is dark enough, we will skip, and when I say, 'Run,' don't stop one moment. Run for your life!"

The boys tried to rest, knowing they needed all the strength they had for later. But the anxiety of the moment, with its dangers and uncertainty, did not let them relax.

The wind began blowing from the north, and dark-looking clouds came rolling ahead of the wind. Then the storm broke upon them.

Hans shivered, not so much from the wind and rain, but from the danger they were in.

The rain came faster. Hans parted the hay to get a view of the village. "It will get dark early," he told Heinerich. "Just listen! It's pouring out there. You can't even see the woods. But we know the direction we want to go even if we cannot see."

Suddenly Hans pushed the hay aside again. "Listen! That's a truck, a military truck, and it's coming up the road toward the boarding house."

He watched a few moments. "Heinerich, look. Not only one military truck, but five or six," he whispered, as if they could hear him above all the noise of the pouring rain and the grinding motors of the military trucks.

"The time is here to beat it for the woods, Heinerich." Hans took Heinerich's arm, half dragging him out into the beating rain.

The terrorized boys were soaked at once. They ran as they had never run before. The rain poured against their faces, as if it were being pitched by the bucketfuls. They had to hold their hands over their mouths and noses to keep from drawing in too much water. They were soon gasping for breath. Still they ran on.

Soaked to the skin, the boys plopped down on the water-soaked ground as they entered the woods and tried to catch their breath.

It was a cold rain, and the boys lay but a few moments, for they soon chilled.

"We are not safe yet," Hans panted, getting to his feet. "They have powerful searchlights, you know!"

Silently the two pushed on, farther and farther into the woods and away from the village before they dared rest again.

The water squashed and sloshed in their boots, while the drenched trees and undergrowth kept dumping water onto them with every step. But their eyes were becoming adjusted to the darkness, and they began to feel more secure. Soon they began to look for a favorable place to rest.

"Let's check this leaning rock over here. I don't think any police will venture out here in this weather. We can rest if we can find a place that is fit," Hans suggested.

The rock indeed proved to be a refuge for them. They found dry leaves under the lower back side. Taking off their heavy, wet outer garments, they hung them on a ledge under the rock and buried themselves in the leaves. They lay close together for warmth. "In times like these, I wish I knew God like my mumsy used to, Heinerich. She trusted in God and taught us to return good for evil. Do you think she would still say so? It's so hard to trust and have faith in these times of murder, war, and greed. You know our end could be near. Then what?"

"I wish I knew, Hans. But why would a God let the government cause so much suffering and trouble? Do you really believe there is one?"

"I'm certain there is, but somehow I can't get faith like Mumsy had. But let's pray that we might find help some way."

Hans swallowed the tears that wanted to rise. Where was Netta? Did she pray for him? Would he ever see her again? And Elly and Lenchen? He had not found Art and Matina. Were they still alive? Were they suffering too?

Aloud, he said, "I know it is hard to have faith when things just go wrong and you are chased like an animal, but let's not give up. Surely, help will come sometime, Heinerich."

But Heinerich was snoring, and Hans, with a tiny seed of faith deep within, prayed softly, "Our Father . . ." But before he had finished, he went to sleep too.

When they awoke, the rain had stopped, and a waning moon hung low in the sky.

"Let's travel east and see if we can find a village or train station," Hans suggested.

It was sunup before they came to the edge of the woods. "We cannot walk out before dark, but the sun feels good, and I believe over against that rise there are some railroad tracks," Heinerich said. "If we'd walk those, our clothes would dry at least, and perhaps there would be some food around those areas too."

"Good idea," Hans said. "Let's investigate."

Heinerich was right. They found the railroad. The warm sun cheered them, but they were getting hungry as they walked slowly down the tracks.

"We could board a train along here," Hans said. "But it likely would have too much speed if it's not near a station."

"No, we'd better walk on," suggested Heinerich. "If we could only get a bite to eat."

"Yes, but there is none here. We must keep going. I hope we are going the right direction."

Several times they rested. The area seemed to be desolate.

"Look!" Hans stopped and pointed to his left. "A man with a team, hauling wood from that piece of woodland. A dwelling must not be far off."

The two struck out across the fields. They could now see that the man had a flowing white beard and that he saw them coming. He stopped his team and waited.

"Let's get acquainted with this grandpa," Hans said, stepping faster.

The elderly man proved to be friendly and very helpful.

The boys explained their needs and asked if he knew of any work they might find.

"Jump on, and we will see if my lady has any food on hand," the farmer said cheerfully. "You may sleep in my barn until night. Then you may want to catch a freight. I'll explain later."

Hans and Heinerich thanked the man warmly, waiting outside while he went inside.

"You know these peasants have a heart, Heinerich. And most of them would be satisfied if the government would leave them alone," Hans said thoughtfully. His thoughts went back to his father's farm and how Mumsy used to send food and clothes to the poor. Now he was in need of someone sharing with him. It humbled him, and he bowed his head in silent prayer. "Thank You for kind people, and help us, God."

The old man brought them bread and a bit of cheese.

"Thank you, thank you, grandpa," the two cried in unison.

The man then told them where they could go, drawing a map with a few directions.

Finished with their meal, the boys lay down on the hay and slept soundly.

Heinerich shook Hans. "Hey, it is dark. Shouldn't we be on our way? We might miss the freight grandpa told us about."

Hans roused himself with difficulty. His legs were cramped and stiff from his long trek through the cold rain. He stretched himself, swinging his legs to get some circulation going. Taking up his coat, he prepared to go.

"What's this in my pocket?" Hans asked, digging out a package. "Bread! These good people did not send us away empty-handed." Their kind thoughtfulness brought tears to Hans's eyes.

The boys caught the freight after midnight, just like the aged man had said. The night air was cold, and they clung to each other, shivering. "Let's lie flat with our feet toward the front," Hans suggested through chattering teeth. It helped, but they were glad when the train slowed for the town of Kurgan and they could walk again. It was twenty miles to the resort the grandpa had told them about.

The resort had mineral baths, and many sick and elderly people came to the baths at that time of year, making it necessary to hire extra workers. The boys looked unkempt to apply for work. Yet many others were shaggy and unkempt too.

Chapter 9

THE PASS

———

*H*ans and Heinerich were extremely tired and weak from hunger by the time they reached the resort. Having gone the wrong direction once and needing to keep hidden, they had traveled extra miles. When they were near enough, they mingled with others traveling the same direction. Hans liked to travel with crowds to avoid suspicion when possible. But he was always alert and in suspense of being taken.

The people they mingled with looked undernourished too, and the boys' dirty clothes did not so easily identify them as fugitives.

As the grandpa had predicted, they found work readily. The pay was not much over their keep, but it kept them from starvation, and with careful spending, they even accumulated a little savings.

Helping the aged around the pleasant grounds and through the long halls of the buildings often put a few coins into Hans's pocket. Hans learned to know many of the patients personally and it proved relaxing to his taut nerves.

Hans also learned to know a friend who was in the military. After hearing Hans's history, this man promised to be on the alert for any danger.

The boys worked here until the spring of 1935. At that time, the government set out to take all Germans. "They are scheduled to make a raid through here soon," the military friend told Hans. "It is no longer safe to stay here. Sorry, pal. I wish it were different," he whispered one evening.

Hans made plans with Heinerich to meet him in town the next day. His military friend had told him the raids were normally made at night so people would not be aware of what was happening.

Having purchased a few basics, Hans waited in the alley for Heinerich. They had planned to walk from the village in the dusk of the evening and hide in a wooded area a few miles away until after midnight. It was time to go, yet Heinerich had not come. Hans waited impatiently, and his taut nerves tightened. Would he come?

The town clock struck nine. Hans could wait no longer. He had perhaps waited too long already. With swift steps he traveled the back alleys and roads until he had left the town behind.

When Hans finally found the railroad tracks, he did not know exactly where he intended to go. He still hoped that Heinerich would show up. Maybe he would have a suggestion. Hans hid in the grass and weeds to think while he waited for a freight. He heard the distant whistle and the vibration of the tracks.

Hans sat up, listening carefully and searching the area for safety. *The train is coming from the south and heading north,* he thought. *That's in the direction of Kiev, near to Elly. Why not?* His heart longed to see her. *Is it safe?* He knew it wasn't, but where would it be safe? There was no such place. Lying flat, Hans awaited the approaching freight which was now slowing down for the next city.

Elly was overjoyed to see Hans but feared for his safety.

"We have not heard of Lenchen for a long time and don't know her whereabouts. I'm afraid she is taken. I know she seriously considered trying to flee the country," Elly explained.

"She might have gone down to the Caucasus to find the others," Hans suggested. "I could not find them, and it is not safe anywhere if you have German blood pumping through your veins, Elly.

"Do you hear anything of Netta?" Hans asked wistfully, his eyes filling with tears. "How I've longed for her in my loneliness."

"No, nothing." Elly wept with Hans. "Lenchen and I visited her before you had to flee, but I have not heard of her since. She, too, might be taken. You cannot trust your friend or neighbor. People will betray you for a few slices of extra bread. They are so desperate for food, they lose common reasoning."

"This I well know, Elly, and I . . . well, I hoped you could help me with my weak faith somehow. You know, like Mumsy used to believe." Hans fumbled for the right words. "Elly, do you believe in God, like you used to? I . . . "

Elly looked troubled. "I do, Hans, but . . ." She dropped her head, wiping her tears with her sleeve. "I do, Hans," Elly repeated, looking pleadingly at him. "But I cannot reach out to Him for faith and strength as I did when I was a girl. It seems my heart is cold, Hans. It scares me. We have no church or ministers, no Bible to read, no Mumsy to show us the way." Elly hung her head and wept brokenly. "All one sees is hate and abuse and cruelty. How can one believe?"

"I know what you mean, Elly. I had hoped somehow you would still hold to that faith and . . . and could help me," Hans stammered.

"So you didn't find Art and Matina?" Elly changed the subject which seemed so fruitless.

"No, no trace of them, but you must remember it was not a fair search. I had to always be alert and on the run."

Hans stayed only three days. He dared not try to see Netta. It would be too great a risk to travel there. Even here, there was danger of being caught or of bringing suspicion on Elly and Bart. So he bid Elly a tearful good-bye, saying he hoped they would meet again.

Hans again boarded a freight at night. The train brought him to a village where lived some friendly Jews. They were kind and willing to hide him and to give him some work with pay.

Some days they would tell Hans, "Today you cannot stay here." Then they would give him a message on paper to deliver to the other end of the village. Thus they shifted him about to avoid being caught in their territory.

Here Hans had refuge for eighteen months. He learned of an aged Jew living there who took special interest in the boys they protected. He had had some success in purchasing new passes for some of them. The new ones did not have the stamp of the Wolf's Pass. Hans approached the kind gentleman about getting a new one for him.

"I can try, Hans," the old man said kindly. "It will take some time and two hundred rubles."

Hans had saved up some money in spite of the adverse circumstances. He knew he could trust the kind Jew with the money, so he handed the needed rubles to him. "It will be worth that to receive a free pass, one that is not contaminated with the old wolf," Hans stated with some of his former humor. Just the thought of getting a free pass made him joyful.

Some time elapsed before the old Jew took the trip to the city. Hans waited with great anticipation, hopeful, and yet with some doubts. It seemed too good to be true.

When the elderly gentleman came home, he told Hans he had no pass because now they asked four hundred rubles.

Hans was greatly disappointed. He had more rubles, which he would gladly give for a clear pass, but he did not have the full amount. "What can I do now?" he asked, feeling more discouraged than he had in weeks.

"Don't worry. Someone will loan you the money. After you have a clear pass, you can get a job and pay back the debt," the old gentleman explained.

Hans was grateful to be among such gracious people who went beyond their obligations to help him. They cared for him as though he were a brother.

Considerable time elapsed before the old man had everything in readiness to get the pass changed. There was so much red tape connected with it that Hans almost despaired. But the old Jew told him not to give up.

Hans waited in suspense and almost fear, the day the Jew went to the city with his pass and the papers they had filled out. First, his hopes would run high. Then he envisioned the other extreme. This might be a means for the officers to locate him. The day seemed to stretch out endlessly.

The old Jew showed Hans the reports. "They say you must apply in person, Hans. I tried to get them to think differently, but I see no other way. Prepare yourself to go."

Hans was discouraged, but decided since he had come this far, he would try. On the train, he wavered. *Will the police be at the other end, ready to grab me? Have the Jews after all betrayed me? No*, he thought, *they have been too helpful and kind.*

Did he imagine that the other passengers on the same coach looked at him suspiciously? Even the conductor examined his ticket twice, peering over his specs to inspect him. Though he rode in suspense, he tried to appear calm.

The five blocks to the courthouse were torture. There were officers at every corner, but seemingly, they had no reason to stop him or question him.

Hans waited at the end of the long line of people outside the door. Most of them were women. The two officers at the door interviewed each one, and some were turned away. A few were permitted to enter.

For two hours Hans waited. The line was still long, and he was no more than halfway to the door. Looking about, Hans saw a side door through which an officer passed. A few others went in that way too, perhaps workers. Hans decided if he could not get in some way, he would miss his ride home and would have to hide in the city that night.

No harm to try, he told himself, walking around to the side entrance. An officer was guarding this entrance also, but no one was waiting outside.

Walking briskly up the walk, Hans nodded at the officer, who stopped him, telling him there was no admittance here.

"I have only a question to ask," Hans said, trying to keep his voice firm and fearless, though he was quaking inside. "I'll be right out again."

To Hans's surprise, the officer stepped aside and let him enter.

Hans saw at a glance to which desk he must go to receive his pass. His heart sank when he saw the surly officer behind the desk. He would have sooner fled than meet this man, but his needs were too pressing. Squaring his shoulders in determination, he walked up to the desk.

Hans waited a moment before the officer took any notice of him.

Giving Hans a quick once-over, he boomed with a voice of authority, "How did you get in here?"

Hans motioned toward the door through which he had entered.

"Who are you looking for, and what do you want?" he bellowed, leaning forward. With cold, piercing eyes he glared at Hans as if he could see through him.

Hans's knees felt weak, but he did not flinch. Without wavering, he stated firmly, "I want to see you, about . . ."

"You what?" roared the officer, his face flaming with anger.

Hans kept his eyes focused on the officer. He had come for his pass, and he was determined not to go without it, having paid double for it.

He waited a moment before he calmly answered, "I came for my . . ."

The officer lowered his voice to a whisper. "You came for your pass?" he questioned.

"Yes, sir."

"Name, please."

"Johann Reimer."

The officer opened a drawer and in a few moments handed Hans his pass.

"Leave the city before night," the officer told him in an undertone, "before anything can be traced back to this office."

Hans accepted the pass from the officer's hands with grateful thanks, nodding to his instructions. He wondered how a person could change not only his voice, but his personality, in such a short time.

"Now get out of here," the officer bellowed in a voice that echoed through the high-ceilinged room.

Hans needed no second bidding. He slipped the pass inside his pocket and left through the side door, thanking the officer on guard outside.

Hans did not delay, but walked to the train station with a light step and a thankful heart.

No longer was he branded with a Wolf's Pass. He was a free man, eligible to get a job with pay.

Hans consulted with the Jew who had befriended him and had helped him receive his clear pass.

"I think it would be well if you could get work elsewhere," the elderly man suggested kindly. "We have others in need also, and we should give those a chance too. Men are coming in faster than they leave, and it makes it all the harder to keep them hidden and supported."

Hans remembered the place of the baths. He was certain he could get work there. He had liked both the work and the location. Many people would be there who needed help. He would at least give it a try.

Hans had no problem finding work at the summer resort. He soon had his debts paid and was saving up rubles for future use.

After working there a year, Hans's thoughts turned to Netta. Was she still living at the place he had last seen her? He had not heard anything about her for nearly eight years. He decided he would write and find out.

Chapter 10

NETTA AGAIN

———

Mail was slow, but Hans waited and watched anxiously to hear from Netta. Had his letter been lost? Perhaps she did not live there anymore. He must be patient. Surely he would hear one of these days. Still, there was no response.

Thus Hans's thoughts churned the pros and cons for almost six months before he received an answer from Netta.

Hans clasped the letter to his breast before he opened it. Seeing the familiar handwriting brought a greater longing for her.

Hans walked to a private place in the shade of an old oak before he opened the letter. Slowly he read and reread the neatly written lines before folding the sheet. He pressed it to his lips while a tear coursed down his cheeks and dropped onto the letter.

"Oh, Netta," he whispered, "now that I have found you again, I will not give you up."

Opening the letter again, he read for the third time. "Things have been going so bad for us since the time you left, and it has been such a long time too, that I think it would be unwise for us to see each other again. Most of the men are taken, and we could not expect anything different. It would only cause us much sorrow and disappointment."

Netta, however, did express her joy in hearing that he was well and had received a clear pass. She wished him well but asked that he try to forget their former plans. She did not want to have her hopes and dreams dashed again, though she knew he could not have prevented it.

Hans thought he could read between the lines. She cared, but did not trust to admit it. His love for her was renewed, and his longing to see her was even greater than before.

Hans wrote again. "For me the times have been bad too, Netta. Could we not face life's trials together, instead of each having to go his way alone?" He expressed his love for her as ever new, and he pleaded that she reconsider and at least let him come to see her. Perhaps they could iron out the difficulties and understand each other better than by writing.

It took, however, several more letters over several more years before Netta agreed to let him come to see her.

Hans had also been corresponding with Elly, and now he wrote to her that he was coming to see Netta and that he hoped she could get a few days off from work to come to see him.

Mutti and Netta's brother, with a few of their friends, pleaded with Netta to change her mind, and receive Hans as her betrothed. But Netta would not listen to their well-meant advice.

"Just think, Netta, what a long wait Hans has had — almost ten years. And you had promised," Netta's brother admonished kindly. "He has had some rough going and has endured many hardships. Yet he remained faithful. How can you turn him down?"

"I realize it's been long. Too long!" Netta answered sadly. "It's not as if I had chosen another to take Hans's place. I have decided to stay single, which is better than to marry and have your husband taken from you. Have I not seen many heartbroken wives, stricken with great grief and sorrow when their husbands were taken?"

However, as the time of Hans's arrival drew near, some of the old expectations and love warmed Netta's inner feelings. She tried not to admit those feelings to herself and was careful not to show her anticipation to her family. Still her smiles told them more than she realized.

Netta received Hans gladly and with sincere respect. But he could not change her way of thinking.

"I am no longer a young girl," she told Hans rather shyly. "And I cannot forget my shattered dreams, though we could not have avoided them."

"True, Netta. My dreams and desires were also shattered," Hans said softly. "Only you can know how it grieved me to leave you. But my love for you has not been shattered, dear. Cannot you trust me again?"

"It is not a question of trusting you, Hans. It's the circumstances. Mutti is getting older, and I need to take care of her. I still have the bookkeeping job, and it would be risky to stop my job and move south as you suggested. One cannot follow the heart these days but must do what is best according to reasonable thinking."

"I'll not keep you late, Netta. You need your rest so you can work in the morning. I'll go back to the beach for the night, but please consider what I have told you. I will come back tomorrow evening."

Netta gave Hans her hand as she said good-bye. "I'll be looking for you," she said softly, dropping her eyes before his gaze. "But please try to understand."

Hans smiled. "I do understand, dear, and it makes me want you more than ever."

Hans crept back to the beach, keeping in the shadows as much as possible, his eyes and ears ever alert to any noise or movement that could mean danger. His heart sang, and he was not discouraged at Netta's refusal. *She cares.* Hans smiled in the dark. *She cannot hide it. I will woo her as in the former days until she cannot refuse.*

Elly visited Hans at the beach. They embraced each other and wept as it brought back many memories. "It is so good to see you again, Hans," Elly smiled through her tears. "At times I thought I would never see any of the family again."

"It is good to see you, Elly. Lenchen never showed up again, did she?" Hans asked sadly.

"No, and none of the others did either."

"Netta's Mutti planned a picnic here at the beach tomorrow, Hans, in honor of your coming home. That's thoughtful of her, is it not, Hans?" Elly continued. "And I am here too to enjoy the day."

"That is nice," Hans said warmly. "I hope Netta can have off from her work that day."

"I'm sure she can, or Mutti would not have planned it."

The day of the picnic proved to be an ideal one for the small group that gathered at the beach for the occasion. The picnic lunch did not consist of what was usually brought, but Mutti managed to bring a few special treats for Hans's sake.

The meager lunch was spread on a clean linen cloth, and the group gathered around to eat. "Elly has an announcement to make before we eat," Mutti told the group, handing her a written note.

Elly could not suppress a smile as she read the note, announcing Hans and Netta's engagement.

With openmouthed astonishment, Netta searched the merry faces turned her way. Blushing a deep crimson, she stammered, "I . . . ah . . . I have not even said yes yet."

As the fullness of their plot struck home, the scheme suddenly appeared humorous to Netta. Covering her face with her hands, she shook with laughter.

The others laughed with her, and the congratulations were passed.

Hans watched her hopefully. She had not refused to accept the announcement. She did not get angry or unhappy about the trick they had played on her. He walked to her side.

"Is it true, Netta?" he asked softly.

"If the others say so, it must be," she whispered, raising her blushing face to meet his gaze. "They pulled a trick on us, did they not?" Netta smiled, and merriment lit her eyes.

"Yes, but it was a nice trick this time," he answered, smiling back. "Now let me fill your plate. Then, will you eat with me?"

Netta nodded her answer, and the light in her eyes told Hans what he wanted to know.

After the picnic a few friends welcomed Hans to join them in the village. "Not now," he told them. "I feel safer out here on the beach."

"I'll be in to see you later this evening," Hans confided to Netta, "as soon as the noises in the village quiet down."

"Do be careful," Netta said with concern. "You never know when the officers may make their raids."

"I'll be careful, Netta. Not only for my sake, but for yours too."

"I'll wait up for you," she whispered, "should it be late." With a wave of her hand, she joined the others who were waiting for her.

Hans watched her slender form as she gracefully walked back toward the village. *I must be every inch a man,* he thought, *to be worthy of such a gentle, beautiful girl.* To him, she looked as young as she had ten years ago.

Time passed slowly for Hans after Netta and the others had left.

Walking up and down the beach, he kept his eyes and ears alert. If he would be taken now that he and Netta had renewed their engagement, it would cause great sorrow. Hans knew since he was a German it would take keen thinking and wise moves to evade the police. He had been successful so far, and he hoped to further escape their treacherous traps. If only the turmoil and the ugly communist head could be quieted down, how different it would be!

His thoughts went again to Papa and Mumsy. *Papa's riches fled like water over a falls. There was no security in them. I trust the security Mumsy had more.* Had it been her dying prayer that had kept him all these trying years when others were taken? It comforted Hans to think it could be so.

Darkness crept over the land while dark shadows filtered across the rippling waters of the lake. Hans was still keeping a lone vigil, slowly tracing his steps up and down the shore. The tiny waves, driven by a slight breeze, lapped gently at his feet, making a serene, muffled sound. His thoughts were drawn again to the peaceful times when Mumsy and Papa were still here. *There will be no minister to marry us, nor Mumsy to give her blessings,* Hans thought sadly.

Complete darkness erased the shadows across the lake, but the peaceful sound of the wavelets remained. The barking of the dogs and the commotion of the village reached Hans's ears very plainly. He could not attempt to go to Netta until all was quiet. *There will not be any moon until after midnight, which will help,* he thought.

Hans was tempted to sneak into the village as things began to quiet down, but Netta had warned him to be very careful, so he waited awhile.

The dogs began to bark anew. *Is there possibly a raid, causing such a ruckus in the village?* Hans waited for it to become quiet again.

It was midnight before he knocked softly on Netta's back door.

Though Hans had thought of the possibility of a raid, he was not prepared to meet the teary-eyed faces he saw inside. The military had raided the village and had taken most of the men, including Netta's brother and uncle. *Tante* Luci and Netta's sister-in-law sat arm-in-arm, mingling their tears and griefs together.

For some time the room was quiet, with the exception of the sobs and prayers that flowed freely for the parted loved ones.

They all realized how cruelly the prisoners were beaten at times and the hardships they would have to endure in prison or at the concentration camps in Siberia, working in the mines where they faced sub-zero weather and near star-vation. After trying to console each other, most of them retired for the night.

Chapter 11

HEADING SOUTH

N etta faced Hans with serious eyes. "You now realize why I hesitated to marry? But since it is now planned, I think we should go ahead as soon as possible. Since our relatives are all gone, we need not wait until they can attend."

"I understand, Netta, and I think it is a wise plan to get married right away and move south. I had hoped Elly might be present, but she was just here on a visit and will not be able to have another day off right away."

"There is little hope of having a home in these parts," Netta said sadly. "But maybe if we go south, you may be spared, at least for some years yet."

Mutti agreed to their plan and made preparations to move south with them, for they had told her they would not leave her behind.

Only a few friends were present to witness the marriage vows of Hans and Netta. They were lawfully married by a justice of the peace. Hans longed to have a minister handle the ceremony as had been the former custom, but none was available to ask.

"If we could only find one to give us the blessings," Hans confided to Netta, who now stood by his side as a new bride. "I feel we need God's blessings on our trip south and always."

"But there is none here," she whispered.

"Why don't we ask Mutti, Netta? She knows how the blessings were said, doesn't she?"

In the privacy of their home, Hans and Netta stood with bowed heads while Mutti clasped their hands together and gave them the blessing. Hans's inaudible prayer from deep within followed the blessing, and he voiced a sincere "Amen" when she was finished.

Hans longed as never before for Mumsy to add her blessings too. Then he remembered she had given her blessings the evening she died. *I may still claim that for this occasion,* Hans thought. For Hans this was a very solemn and holy occasion.

Ten people were invited to the marriage supper. Mutti somehow managed to have a thin borscht. It being June, some vegetables were available, but they were still hard to find. She also had fruit and a sweet cake.

However, with the sad situation of their time, only a few hymns were sung before the guests took their leave, wishing the newly-wedded couple a peaceful married life. Each one was aware that trials and persecution would most likely be their lot.

Netta tried to get a release from her bookkeeping job, but they would not accept her plea. When all efforts failed,

Hans and Netta thought the best plan would be for Netta to keep up the work at the office until the day of their departure, and then they would go in secret. It was risky, but so was anything else.

They needed to go to the big city first and take a train headed southeast. Only one train per day traveled that route, and they did not think it safe to stay in the city long, so Hans tried to find the best time to leave.

"We can take with us only what we would take on a trip to visit folks over the weekend," Hans told Mutti, as she was getting things prepared to move.

"I realize that, son," Mutti answered. "There is much we have to leave, but that is better than being taken by the police."

"It is a sacrifice on your part, Mutti, for this trip might not end as we would wish." Hans tried to give Mutti a glimpse of the danger they faced. But Mutti had weighed the possibilities and knew she would be happier to share trouble with Hans and Netta than to live alone with the uncertainty of the times.

If Hans and Netta went alone, she might never hear from them again and wouldn't know if they were dead or alive.

The crowded train station at the large city was in a turmoil as passengers poured in from arriving trains and hurried to board those that were departing.

Netta thought she had never seen so many people at one place. She wondered how they would ever find the right train and the correct gateway leading to it. She and

Mutti sat at one corner of the huge station, waiting for Hans.

They soon saw him striding toward them, weaving in and out among the mob of moving people. He had their tickets, but went on to explain that they were not the ones they had thought to buy.

"There is no room today on the train we wanted, and I thought it was not safe to stay here overnight, so I decided to buy tickets to North Junction. This will take us out to the lakes, where we may get a boat to take us south. We may board a train later for the South Steppes."

Netta did not understand it all and thought it quite queer that they should board a train that would take them farther away from the Steppes, but she trusted Hans's decision. "Perhaps we can make it our wedding trip," she said, smiling at Hans when they were seated in the coach. "It's kind of a thrill to think of a boat ride."

"I suppose so, but it will be a solemn one and filled with danger. No telling how soon the office reporter where you worked will put the police on our trail."

The train started to move, and Hans was relieved when he saw several police boarding the other train. They were inspecting the passengers and their tickets as they boarded.

"We made it in time," Hans whispered to Netta. "I'm glad we were on this train before the police arrived."

"Thank the Lord," Netta whispered, clasping her hand to her heart. "Will there be a stop between here and North Junction?"

"There will be two, but both are only small places, like North Junction."

"Couldn't they be there too?"

"They could, but it is not likely," Hans answered, taking a deep breath. He tried to assure Netta, but he knew there still was danger lurking wherever they would go.

"There is a store," Hans told Netta when the train stopped at the last station before they would reach North Junction. "Perhaps I can find something to eat. We will need food to take along on the boat."

Netta wished he would not need to go away but knew what he said was true. Besides, she had a headache and thought some food might help to get rid of it.

Hans had not stepped from the car long before a military police came down the aisle, checking tickets and getting the information he wanted.

Netta's heart skipped a beat, but she knew she needed to remain composed. She concentrated on fixing the thin rope that tied the bundle on her lap and gave no sign of noticing the officer until he spoke.

"Your tickets, please," he said with marked authority, holding out his hand to receive them.

Netta looked up into the face of the scowling officer. How she wished Hans were here, yet without any hesitation, she answered, "My husband left the coach a minute ago to get a few things to eat. He has the tickets."

"Where are you going?" the same stiff voice asked.

"To North Junction," Netta answered truthfully.

"Your mission?"

Netta thought she could feel the heat of the officer's breath on her hair as he bent closer as if to inspect her better. "We want to visit my sister. My mother," Netta added, patting Mutti's arm.

The officer's scowling face searched Mutti's for a long moment. Then finally satisfied that he knew what was needed, he passed on to the next seat.

Netta hoped the officer had not heard her suppressed breath of relief. She noticed, however, that he glanced out the window several times and toward the door through which Hans had left. She now hoped Hans would not come back while the officer was still in their coach.

With one more glance out the window, the officer made his way into the next coach.

Hans did not come until the train started to move. Netta sat up straight, trying to see through the window on the other side. *Surely they did not pick up Hans before he got inside,* Netta worried. *Why has he not returned?*

Turning, Netta saw him entering the coach, from the other direction.

"Did you see the officer?" Netta questioned as soon as he sat by her side.

"I did, and I thought it would be better to come in the other way," Hans said seriously. "How did you make out?"

"All right, I hope. He questioned us, but finally seemed to be satisfied," Netta said. "But, oh, I feared for you. I was afraid he could read fear in my face, for I was sure I trembled. I tried to remain calm."

"That was the best you could do, Netta." Hans pressed her fingers in appreciation. "I boarded the coach ahead of us with a few others. Then I made my way to this coach as soon as I could."

The rest of the ride was uneventful, and they arrived at North Junction on schedule.

Netta enjoyed the boat ride. The first boat made connections with another which took them nearly twenty-five miles farther south. Here they left the lakes and went inland by rail.

Hans wanted to arrange their journey so they would reach the big city in time to catch the train south but would have very little waiting time.

"I'll have to check if this train will make connections with the train to the Steppes in time today. If not, we want to wait here until tomorrow, instead of in the large city," he explained to Netta.

"Good news," Hans said after checking with the ticket agent. "We will reach the city just twenty minutes before the train leaves for connections farther south."

"Will that give us enough time?" Netta asked.

"Yes, if we have everything ready so we can change trains without going into the depot. Both trains will be on the tracks near the station at one time."

"At least the office back in our village will not have any trace of us, all the crisscrossing we did so far," Netta mused.

"You never know, Netta. I hope they will not cause us any trouble."

Chapter 12

HANS IS TAKEN

———

Netta's sister Mahlia met them at the station. She was both smiling and weeping as she welcomed them with joy.

"Things will be a little different down here from what you were accustomed to," she told Netta. "People in general are poor, but we still have our homes and most of our loved ones are with us yet."

Mahlia had borrowed a wagon and a team to fetch them. "As you can see," she continued, "these steppes are barren unless they are irrigated."

The three weary travelers were welcomed into Mahlia's humble home and given a good warm meal before they talked business.

Mahlia offered enough land for Hans to build a house and raise a small garden. There would also be enough pastureland that they could have a goat.

Hans accepted the offer, bought the plot, and decided to begin building at once.

Netta looked forward to a home of their own. However, it took Hans some time to get enough stones hauled to build the house.

Netta could hardly wait to get started. When Hans was ready, she helped by mixing mortar and carrying the stones for him. However, when Hans could get a few days' work for pay, he had to work to keep them fed.

But by persistent labor and management, they did make progress, and the house began taking on some shape. Still, it was not fast enough to suit Netta.

"Couldn't we move into our house soon?" she asked Hans one evening after a hard day of labor. "We could manage somehow. Then we would not need to pay rent, and you would not have to work away so often," Netta insisted.

"I'm afraid you work too hard, Netta. I suppose we could as soon as I get the roof on. We could move in and finish later. But it may be quite trying. It is a small house for the three of us, and we would still have the dirt and stones around the building. Are you sure you want to?"

And so they found that building a house was just a little more complicated than they had thought. It was not until the spring of 1941 that they finally moved into their own home. They had started in the summer of '39, so it was almost two years. Still, it was not completely finished.

Though their furnishings were few, Netta was happy to have a home of their own. She sang as she worked and planted the garden. Gardening was new work to her, but with Mutti's help and the kind neighbor's advice, she managed to raise food to eat.

The unrest in Russia was spreading out its greedy talons like those of a huge falcon, gripping whatever or whoever came within reach.

"How is it that others are taken," a neighbor woman asked Netta one day while she was harvesting beans from her garden, "and Hans is still here?"

Netta looked up from her work. A worried line creased its way across her brow. "That we don't know," Netta said wearily. "If only he can be spared until the baby comes," she added softly, confiding her secret to her neighbor.

"I'll be glad for your sake if he is, but it is hardly thinkable," she said with pity in her voice.

Netta appreciated her friend's sympathy. The German invasion of Russia put all the Germans living there in great danger. Stalin had ordered all Germans to be taken.

The young men were forced to join the military while the older ones were sent to the mines to work, freeze, or starve. Women were ordered to work on the farms like men. In Siberia the concentration camps were increased as new mines were being dug. The goal was either to work the Germans to death or starve them or both.

Although Russian-born Germans had no part in the invasion, the government said Germans were killing their men and boys, and those within their grasp would pay for it.

Hans and Netta made plans. There was no doubt but that he would be taken any time. Still God intervened.

"Mumsy asked God to take care of us," Hans confided once more to Netta. "It is the only thing that has kept me here. What troubles me, Netta, is that we have no worship services. We know so little about spiritual things. My longing is that God would someway reveal these things to me, that we might do what is right.

"Our lives are in jeopardy, Netta, and what then?"

Netta only shook her head sadly. "Hans, I don't know, but right now my utmost concern is you. If there is a God, may He keep you with us a while yet until the baby comes."

"Somehow I think He will, Netta. Or why have I been spared while so many others have been taken? However, we do need to be prepared to separate. Then, Netta, I trust you will do what you know is right and try to teach our child too. I will do the same."

"We should have some way of sending secret messages, Hans. Always check the stamp to see where the letter was mailed from. Then you will know if we are still here or if we were transferred."

"That is a good idea, and the same with you. Why don't we put a code mark under the stamp. A circle will mean we are well. An X will mean trouble. I know we will not be able to communicate often and that all our letters will be closely checked. Too much information would certainly cause the letter to be destroyed."

Months passed. The baby was a girl. Hans and Netta were delighted, in spite of the dark cloud that hung over them.

"Let's name her Lenchen after your sister," said Netta, cradling the infant lovingly in her arms.

Hans bent over her, smiling. "As you wish, Netta. I thought maybe you would want to name her after your mutti."

"No, I like Lenchen. She is a little Reimer anyway. Not?"

Hans squeezed Netta's hand, and she knew he was pleased with the name.

Another year passed. Still Hans was not taken. Yet they lived in suspense day after day.

Neighbors and friends questioned why he was not taken. Some rejoiced with them while others were envious.

The Reimers tried to make good use of their freedom, or rather, their days together, for nobody lived in freedom these days. The government became more oppressive, and the food became scarcer by the day. Everyone worked for food without thinking of pay.

Lenchen now was two and crowed with delight when Papa came home. He would toss her high and hold her close to himself, always aware that this bliss could not last much longer. He must enjoy her while he could.

Two more years passed. Lenchen was four, and Hans was still privileged to be at home. "God truly is good to us, Netta," Hans said with feeling. "I think we should teach our little one about Him." How helpless they both felt in this duty!

The day came, however, when the officers were sent again to make a complete search for Germans. Hans was taken, and the little heaven on earth came to an abrupt end.

Netta was put to work in the grain fields, digging canals by hand for irrigation. This was also women's work. Netta soon had blisters on her hands and was tired to the bone by the time she came home at night. Still she felt blessed to have Lenchen and Mutti at home when she returned.

A year passed, and Netta had heard from Hans only once. It was just a short note. The paper was so rumpled and the writing so pale from handling that it was hardly readable. *His handwriting looks as if he is weak,* Netta thought as she wet the letter with her tears. *Oh, Hans, we are weak and hungry too.*

Although Netta had Mutti and Lenchen to feed, her allotment of a slice of bread was not increased. And so in the spring when the mushrooms grew, they gathered them with delight. What a treat they were, adding much-needed nourishment as well!

Netta then learned that if she knitted at night, she would receive some extra rations. Of course, she was required to continue working during the day too. Then the day came that Netta had to work away from home. It was too far to return home in the evening, so on weekends she walked home, bringing what little food she could provide for Mutti and small Lenchen. They still had a goat, which brought some nourishment for them when the goat had milk.

Chapter 13

THE MINES

---

*H*ans was loaded into a military wagon and made to ride in back with many others. The rough roads and careless driving jolted them about like a load of animals, testing their weary bodies to the limit. There was nothing to eat, and their stomachs ached with hunger.

On and on they rumbled. Some of the captives swore in pain and fear. Others wept. Anguish was written on every face. Hans was saddened by the thought of leaving his family in a time of need, but he also realized he could have been taken earlier. How he wished the terrible war and unrest would soon be over and he would be able to return and again meet his family's needs. He knew nothing was to be gained by complaining about their unfortunate circumstances, so he tried to cheer his fellow captives. But most of them would not be consoled. A few of them even became angry. So Hans remained quiet and tried to sleep as they rode on into the night.

Morning was dawning when they rode into a town. Here they were herded into a prison where they were held for questioning.

The test was severe. They were made to work in the daytime and were brought in for questioning at night. The food was scarce—only one piece of bread with a bit of water each day. As if this were not enough, the prisoners were not permitted to sleep but were lined up in a row and made to stand all night. This continued for several weeks. The men became so weak they stood against the wall to steady themselves. If they had a piece of paper, they would hold it in front of their faces as though reading and catch a few naps standing up.

"They are weakening us so we will be willing to betray others," Hans told the prisoners who shared the overcrowded cell with him. "But I hope the Lord will give me strength that I may never betray anyone. One of my friends betrayed me for more bread, or I would not be here now."

Sure enough, the next day they were offered more rations if they would betray any hidden German and anyone not in favor of the new administration. Some could not resist. Those who did were cruelly beaten.

"You may kill me," Hans boldly answered them, "but I will not betray anyone."

They cursed Hans and threatened to starve him until he would betray someone. But before they could carry out their plans, a load was scheduled to be sent on to Siberia to work in the mines.

Hans, with a group of others, arrived at a Siberian camp in the evening. They were weary, hungry, and cold, but no warm supper awaited them.

Hans walked to a group of men who were tacking pieces of rubber tires to the bottom of their soles. He watched in silence for some time. *How clumsy those thick soles will be for walking or working. Heavy too,* Hans reasoned. Finally, his curiosity made him ask, "Why do you do that?"

"By tomorrow night you will not only know, but you will be tacking some on your own soles," an aged man answered him.

The first morning Hans went to work the temperature was seventy-eight degrees below zero. The men were not dressed for such extreme temperatures, and Hans's feet were soon frozen beyond feeling.

The ground was frozen six to seven feet deep, and they had to dig in this frozen ground by hand, using shovel and pick, sledgehammer and chisel. These were heavy tools for thin, half-starved men.

Hans saw one of his fellow workers drop, overcome with weakness from starvation and hard labor.

Dropping the pick he was using, Hans went to help the poor man.

"Back to your work," the guard shouted. "He can take care of himself. Or remain there resting sweetly," he added with a hollow laugh.

No one else seemed concerned, and Hans resumed his work, realizing that the government actually intended either to work them, or starve them, to death.

The officers well knew it took only a few minutes for a person to freeze in this sub-zero weather. They also knew death motivated the other workers to keep on digging, in spite of the weariness and cold that enveloped the body and lulled it to drowsiness.

Hans was tacking strips of tires to his shoes when he recognized Andi sitting among the men around the stove. The two embraced, weeping.

Poor Andi! In the few years since Hans had seen him, he had turned into an old man. He was visibly sick and starved.

Hans did not think Andi would have to go to work the next morning, but he was ordered to go.

Hans worked side by side with Andi, encouraging him and trying to dig for them both, knowing if Andi fell, he would freeze to death.

Andi barely survived the day, and Hans and a fellow worker supported him back to the camp.

Hans was determined that Andi would see a doctor that evening. Surely the doctor would order Andi to the hospital. *Then he will not need to go to work tomorrow,* Hans thought, helping Andi to the canteen where the soup would be served.

Hans was disgusted. They were again being served prickly nettle soup. The black soup was salty and bitter as gall. The men could not eat it. Weary and hungry, they stumbled away to rest by the fire.

Andi ate a small portion of the soup, hoping to fill the empty, aching spot in his stomach, but it only made him feel more sick.

"Come, Andi. We are going to see a doctor," Hans said, taking his arm and half dragging the weak, starved man.

"Andi needs to see a doctor," Hans pleaded, boldly meeting the eyes of the grim officer who answered his knock. "He has been sick all day, and for some time — too sick to work."

The redness in the bleary eyes of the officer and the smell of drink on his breath told Hans he had been drinking excessively.

"Ha, ha," the officer laughed rudely, addressing the other officers in the room. "We have two lazy buzzards here who want to see a doctor."

"Yes, please. Just for . . ."

Again the officer laughed hilariously. Then he swore and pointed a shaking finger at Hans and Andi. "You two need more work, not a doctor!"

Hans made another attempt to plead for mercy, but the officer shoved them rudely out the door, banging it shut.

Oh, heartless and unmerciful! Hans groaned inwardly, grieving for Andi. Silently Hans prepared a bed beside the stove for Andi. "I'll stay with you tonight, Andi," Hans said tenderly, covering him with his own coat, which he actually needed himself to keep warm.

Hans carried in more wood and kept the fire going. *Perhaps if I keep him real warm, he will feel better in the morning,* Hans reasoned to himself, *but it looks hopeless.*

A few of the men came close and looked at Andi's pale, drawn face, shaking their heads sadly.

Hans checked Andi again, put more wood into the stove, and then tried to sleep, knowing he needed the rest to work the next day.

He dozed fitfully, then woke with a start. *The stove needs more wood,* he thought. But he found he could only push in a few sticks. He had not slept long. Still half asleep, he bent low to check Andi and found life had fled.

Hans grieved over Andi's dead body. *If only there would be a minister here to have a short funeral sermon,* he thought sadly.

Taking up the coat he had covered Andi with, he put it on. *Andi will not be needing it any longer,* he mused, a tear sliding down his cheeks. Almost he wished he could have died with Andi, but his thoughts went back to Netta and Lenchen. They needed him. Would he ever see them again?

Hans seldom heard from Netta, but his thoughts were with her and Lenchen continually. He knew Netta had to work hard for the government and that food was scarce for them too. Could they survive?

Thus the years passed. Hans always was cheered by Netta's short letters, especially when he looked under the stamp and found a circle. It meant they were existing at least. He would make a circle too, before placing the stamp. It was their way of secretly communicating. Each of them cherished the unwritten message it contained.

"What a waste of food," Hans exclaimed with disgust, as he watched a load of frozen potatoes being dumped on the ground in a pile outside the barracks. His mouth watered for the potatoes. How much nourishment the men could have had, if they had been made into soup! But the only way they were served was in their frozen state. Even then they were delicious, compared to the prickly nettle soup.

Food became so rotten and scarce at camp that the men pulled grass, dug roots, ate anything that would quiet in part the hunger pangs and keep them alive.

After Andi died, Hans was more serious-minded and longed for a better knowledge of God. *Did Andi know God? Is he now in Heaven?*

Hans knew he could easily have the same fate, for not a day had gone by without some worker's death. He also realized that some were not Christians. Didn't God care? Why was there so much suffering and war? If he only had a Bible to read. Thinking of Mumsy and her Bible, he tried to pray. No words came, but surely God heard his inner- most plea for wisdom and his longing to know Him.

Chapter 14

SICKNESS

They try to starve us to make room for others, Hans thought as he watched several truckloads of men being unloaded. *They may not be quite as thin as we are, but they certainly are not well-fed, and some look sickly.* His heart went out to them, knowing what they would experience here.

Hans realized his strength and health were failing as well as his reasoning ability. His stomach felt as if it had been fused together. He needed something to fill it. Drinking more water was the only means of refueling. He realized he could drink too much, yet could not resist the continuous call of his body for food.

Work seemed to him more strenuous and impossible each day. He would not be able to go on much longer unless God intervened.

Hans thought again of Andi and the reality of death. *Then what?* He could not erase the seriousness of the afterlife from his mind.

Hans stumbled home with much effort. Could he possibly go to work the next day? He knew if he lived until morning, they would force him to. But if he went, would he be able to return? Or would he fall and join the others who had fallen that day?

"Nettle soup!" Hans whispered in disgust. "I cannot eat it; it makes me sick even to smell it."

In a daze he stumbled to the water pump outside. It would help soak up the dry thin piece of bread that would be his supper tonight.

Drinking slowly, Hans rubbed his oversized stomach. He realized it was expanding from drinking too much water. *I am as round as a barrel,* he thought absentmindedly.

Feeling faint and miserable, Hans groaned inwardly. In an audible voice he cried, "Lord, look down and have mercy."

The head cook had come outside to pitch out some water in time to hear Hans's groan. He noticed his bloated stomach.

"Hey, buddy," he called, walking up to Hans.

Hans was startled from his reverie, not knowing what he had done wrong.

"Come with me, buddy," the cook said, taking hold of Hans's arm. "You have been drinking too much water into that empty stomach."

Hans stumbled after the cook, not knowing or caring what became of him. Faintly in the back of his mind, Netta appeared. He groped to get a clearer view of her, but swooned away as the cook laid him into a bed.

"I just put a patient into a hospital bed," the cook told

the doctor. "He may not be alive any longer by the time you get there."

"I'm busy right now, but I'll at least check him some-time tonight," the doctor answered absently. Cases like this were frequent, and often were too late for medical help. The doctor was hardened to it.

The cook left the hospital in disgust, swearing under his breath. "Too late, no doubt. I wish I would not need to see another death or another starvation," he muttered to himself. "Many could be avoided if I were permitted to cook for the prisoners as I do for the officers." His fists tightened, but he knew it would not be healthy for him to let others hear his viewpoints.

Hans waited for a letter from Netta. He had lost track of time when he was sick. But now that he was beginning to improve, he longed to know how things were going at home. When the letter came, it was short and badly written. Hans detected that all was not well. He worked at the stamp care-fully, to remove it without destroying the thin envelope. There was no sign at all, neither an X nor a circle. And there was no explanation.

Tears flowed as Hans thought of Netta being sick or perhaps starving. "Surely some great trouble has come to her since she did not use any of our codes," he reasoned. His longing to go to her increased sevenfold. Yet he knew it was impossible. Again he groaned inwardly, *Great God, forgive and have mercy.*

Rereading the letter every day, Hans tried to find some clue he might have missed. He scrutinized every corner in hopes of finding something, but found nothing. *Her handwriting, which was always so neat, is shaky,* he thought. *She did not say she is helping in the harvest, but wrote that harvest is underway. Indeed, something is amiss. Will I ever see her again?*

Taking out his identification card, Hans opened the pocket that held Netta and Lenchen's photos. His whole being filled with love and longing as he gazed at them. How well-fed and nourished they appeared on these photos. *But how do they look now?*

Suppressing a sob, Hans's eyes filled with tears. He wiped them away in an effort to look at the photos again before replacing them.

"May I have those a moment?" a voice asked softly above his bed.

Hans was startled. He trusted no one in these parts, and he did not wish to lose the only connection he had with Netta. He pressed the photos to his breast, and was about to refuse the request.

"May I look at them for a moment?" the voice repeated kindly.

Hans now realized it was the doctor speaking, and he was holding out his hand to receive them. Reluctantly, Hans handed them over.

"My cousin, Netta," the doctor stated firmly, handing the photos back to Hans. "At first I thought it was someone who resembled her, but it is Netta."

Hans was astonished. "She is my wife," he said in a hushed, reverent tone.

The doctor came around to the front of the bed. He shook hands with Hans. "Glad to meet you, Cousin Hans. My mother and hers were sisters. It has been many years since we met. Netta told me then she was betrothed, but that her friend had to flee."

"That is true. I was gone ten years until my pass was cleared and I could come back to Netta. Under very trying circumstances we were finally married. Now we have a little girl and I am here." Hans wiped his eyes again.

After that day, the doctor visited Hans more often, being very sympathetic and friendly which did much to lift Hans's spirits.

Hans also received better food, which he credited to the doctor's orders.

Under the pleasant care of his friendly doctor, Hans gained fast. He was able to get out of bed, yet all about him he saw misery and starvation. How he longed to be able to help others in their suffering!

Hans had now been hospitalized eight months, and he knew that any day the doctor would release him, and he would be sent to dig in the mines on a starvation diet.

With health and strength returning, Hans's mind became clear, and memories of Mutti, Elly, and Netta were renewed. He had heard from Netta only once in that time, and now he longed as never before to go see her. He was certain she was not well, and perhaps not even living anymore.

However, such thoughts were pointless. Even if he included them in his groanings to God, it was unthinkable to actually happen.

The doctor wore a warm smile. "Surprise this morning," he grinned teasingly.

"A what?" Hans brushed his hair from his eyes to see if the doctor had a package or letter from Netta.

The doctor smiled again at the startled, expectant expression on Hans's face.

"I am going to release you. You have recovered nicely. But to bring about a complete recovery, I also bring you a three-month furlough to go home and see Netta and your daughter. Give her my best regards."

Hans could scarcely contain the good news. He fumbled for words of thanks, but the doctor did not wait to hear them. With a farewell salute, he walked out of Hans's life.

Chapter 15

BLOOD POISONING

Netta lost weight, and her strength was tried to the limit as she pitched sheaf after sheaf of grain into the running machine. Today was exceptionally warm and dusty.

Whenever she came off one stack to start another, she would drink water from the pail to quench her burning thirst. *If I could only still the hunger in the same manner, I would have more strength,* she thought.

It was a great relief when the whistle blew, and she could stick her fork in the stack for the day. *If I could only go to Mutti and Lenchen to see how they are making out . . . or better still, if I could but bring them some food!*

Netta realized she could not go home until the threshing season was over. Being eight miles from home, she did not have the strength to walk that far even on Sundays when they were not asked to work. And some weeks, if the harvest was pushing, they were required to work Sundays too.

That night she rested well. And she approached the wheat stack she had left the night before feeling refreshed. She was often surprised her strength held up as well as it did. But she knew that before the day was over, she would be weak and tired enough to drop. *If only the food rations would be more.*

"We finished that stack last night, Netta," one of the women told her. "I guess we start with this one."

"Likely," Netta answered. "The machine is set for it."

The man at the machine was greasing up, in readiness to begin the day, so Netta climbed the stack of wheat, adding more scratches to her bare legs. But she hardly noticed, being used to it.

"Hand me the fork, please," Netta asked one of the workers who was about to ascend the same stack.

Taking the fork, Netta reached the handle back to her to help her climb the stack.

At the same time the engine of the threshing machine started, and a guard appeared to get them going.

"What do you want on that stack?" he bellowed angrily. "Can't you see we want to do this one first?"

Netta did not wait another moment, for the irked officer looked as if he were about to climb the stack she was on and pitch her off.

With fork in hand, she slid to the ground, but in her haste, she scratched her foot on a fork tine. Lifting her foot, she wiped a bit of blood away. *Only another scratch,* she thought. *I've got plenty of those.*

114

"What are you waiting for?" the officer hollered. "Get up on that other stack before I pitch you up there with a fork!"

Netta climbed the stack. Ignoring the burning sensation she felt in her foot, she pitched her first sheaf of wheat for the day.

"He just wanted to show his authority," one of the workers spoke into Netta's ear, above the hum of the threshing machine.

Netta looked about, making certain no officer was near. "Yes, when this stack is finished, we will do that one before they move the machine."

Netta tried to show the scratch on her foot to her helper, while they refreshed at the water pail, but the black dust of the wheat had smeared with the blood, so that it was not visible.

"It still burns a little," Netta told her. "I hope it doesn't amount to anything."

"Be sure to clean it well tonight," the worker advised. "It could be bad if an infection would set in."

Netta again climbed the stack of wheat she had first climbed that morning. *What difference did it make to him which stack we pitched first?* she thought, feeling weak and tired as she reached the top this time. *I would not have scratched my foot on the fork if he had let us alone.*

Exhausted at the end of the day, Netta plumped down on the scattered straw around the edge of the bagger. She would rest a bit before she walked to where she boarded.

The man at the bagger was cleaning up the grain that had been spilled, shoveling it into a waiting grain wagon.

Netta waited, rubbing the dust from her sore foot. *I need to wash it,* she thought. *I hope that will stop the throbbing.*

The man at the bagger left. Only a few of the women remained. Netta scooted closer to the bagger. Farther out from where the man had cleaned, Netta searched through the thinly-scattered straw for a few grains of wheat.

They would just be lost, she reasoned, *and no one would get any good from them. Besides, we work for no wages, and scarcely receive enough rations to keep us from starving.*

Grain by grain, Netta gathered a little handful. She hid the grain inside her garment in a specially prepared pocket. She hoped there would be enough grain gathered by the time harvest was over to make some bread for Mutti and Lenchen. The thought of the aroma of bread baking made her mouth water.

Netta's foot hurt more than she liked to admit when she walked to work the next morning. "I cleaned it the best I could," she told the women that asked her how she was doing. "But not having any warm water or soap to clean it, I'm afraid I did not get the dirt all out. It looked a little red around the scratch."

By the third morning, Netta walked with difficulty. She tried to tell the officer on duty, but he simply brushed her aside without looking at her foot at all.

By that evening, Netta's foot throbbed and pounded. She knew she would not be able to work in the morning.

She again approached the officer in hopes of getting more attention. Sitting down on the ground, she showed him the ugly red streaks that were already showing on her leg.

The officer, however, took little notice and offered no advice or help.

"I will not be able to help with the work until my foot is better," Netta said bluntly. "It hurts too much to be on it; besides I should bathe the sore."

"You can just sit there," the officer answered, walking away. "But remember, there will be no rations unless you work. There are others who will replace you," he added scornfully. "So we need not be concerned."

Netta bathed her foot most of the night, but it got worse by the minute. She was running a temperature, she was certain, and her whole leg began to throb and hurt. It felt hot to her touch.

I might just as well try to make it home to Mutti, Netta decided, though she did not know how she would be able to walk that distance.

Searching for a stick she could use for a crutch, she prepared to walk the eight miles early that morning.

Walking was painful, but with the crutch, Netta thought she could make it. However, her temperature was rising, and by the time she had covered half the distance, her foot ached and throbbed unmercifully. But Netta knew she could not return, nor could she get relief on the way. And so, she kept pushing on, resting frequently.

Her thoughts were drawn anew to Hans. Where was he? No doubt he was suffering too, and needed to work without sufficient food. *Is he still alive? Did he find the way to*

Heaven? Did he learn to know God? Thoughts pressed heavy upon her heart as she lay beside the road, holding her throbbing leg.

Netta realized that without medical aid, her case could be fatal, for she was certain the infection had turned to blood poisoning. If only Hans would be here to teach her the way! Should she die, what then?

Netta had three more miles to go. But she could no longer walk. She had hobbled on one foot with the aid of the crutch the last mile. Now she was too sick and tired to go on.

Reaching into the bag that contained the wheat she had collected over the harvest season, she ate some of the kernels, chewing them slowly. *They will give me some strength,* she thought. But she felt alone and forsaken. No one seemed to travel this road, and there was no help along the way. If her foot had not been hurting so badly, she would have taken a nap.

Netta did not know how long she sat there. Her fever rose to delirium height.

But finally, getting up on all fours, Netta began to crawl the last lap of her journey. *Is that Hans in the distance? Why doesn't he come to me?* She tried to hurry forward but rolled over in the dust instead. "Hans, Hans!" she called, starting forward again. Then she realized she had only imagined a bush in the distance to be Hans. Tears of disappointment slid down her face.

Why doesn't Hans write? Doesn't he receive my letters? Netta wondered as she crawled on, her knees worn through and bleeding from scraping over the rough sand and fine stones. But Netta hardly noticed, for the pain in her foot and leg were greater.

Netta inched on, foot by foot, until finally, with her thoughts roaming with delirium and exhaustion, she crawled into camp, where Mutti and Lenchen met her and took her inside the tent.

Mutti soon had Netta resting on her own grass bed. Netta rolled and moaned in pain. Trying to rise, she called for Hans.

Mutti held her down. She was applying hot packs to the badly discolored leg. However, the heat seemed only to set Netta's leg on fire with pain. She tried to push the warm, wet pads away, screaming, "No! No!" Then she swooned away to unconsciousness.

All through the night, Netta's fever raged. She woke up sensible for only a few moments, in which she tried to tell Mutti what to do when she died. Then she lapsed back into merciful unconsciousness, calling for Hans.

Mutti continued to apply hot packs during the night. When Netta awoke, Mutti tried to force a few spoonfuls of soup between her lips. But Netta refused to eat, saying she would soon die anyway, and Lenchen needed the nourishment.

But Mutti would not give in until Netta had taken a cupful of the hedgehog soup she had prepared for supper.

In Netta's unconscious state, her breathing at times was so soft and low that Mutti had to bend low to catch the faint sound. Was she indeed going to die? Hans and Lenchen needed her. What would she do without Netta? How could she help her now? Hot, silent tears chased each other down her cheeks and dropped onto the hot packs on Netta's leg.

"If I could but get a doctor from the village," she sobbed, "it maybe wouldn't be too late."

Chapter 16

THE GOSPEL

H ans met Otto Hummel and Franz Mueller at the train station. They, too, had leaves to go home.

The officer who brought them to the station handed them their tickets. "This will take you to the first large city. Then you will change trains for your points south."

Without giving them food or money, the officer left the three to wait for their train.

Hans realized they had to walk the last stretch of their journey, perhaps eighteen miles. If they did not have to linger anywhere, he thought he could make it, but his friends, Otto and Franz, had not been privileged with more rations as he had of late, and were hardly in a condition to make the trip. Especially Otto. Tears came to Hans's eyes to see the pathetic condition Otto was in. In spite of his poor condition, Otto's eyes had a sparkle at the thought of going home to see his mother.

When they reached the large city, Hans told his two companions to take seats while he went to see about their connections south.

"Another hour and we will be on our way," Hans said cheerfully to his waiting companions. This brought cheer and smiles to their countenances, for traveling south would bring them near to friends and food.

The three anxious travelers were waiting at the gate when the southbound train was announced to be loading. But when the stationmaster finally came to the gate, he announced that the train was filled. There was not even standing room.

The three men walked slowly back to their seats. "I'll check the schedules again." Hans tried to remain cheerful for his companions' sake. "Perhaps there will be another train going in the same direction soon since this one was full."

Hans was gone a long time. He tried every angle he could in an effort to make some connection to the south. However, their tickets were good only to travel this certain route.

"There is no other train south for twenty-four hours," Hans said, trying to announce the disappointment as mildly as he could. But the brightness left Otto's eyes as if his death sentence had been announced. Hans thought the delay might be just that, but he tried to cheer his companions, saying twenty-four hours would pass quickly. "We will sleep under the benches of the train station," he told them.

Hans was up and walking about the station before the others roused. In one corner, a mother and her two children were eating a roll for their breakfast. Hans watched from a distance until they left. Walking to the place where they had been, he picked up a few crumbs the children had dropped on the floor. Carefully he carried them to Otto. How he longed to buy some food for him, but this was all he had.

Otto licked up the few crumbs, but Hans saw that he was almost too weak to stand. They all walked to the water fountain and filled up with water.

Again the three waited at the gate, thinking they would soon be on their way. Since the stationmaster knew of their disappointment the day before, he would see that they got on the train this time.

Yet the same information reached their ears as the day before. Again there was not even standing room on the train, and they again were turned away from the gate.

Hans was not a little disturbed this time. "If no one else will look into this, I will," he told his companions. "Here we have tickets to ride on this train, and they keep putting us off. Something is wrong. I'm going to call the Kremlin."

With determined steps, Hans walked to the information center and asked to use the phone. After explaining what had taken place, he was promised a reservation on the next day's train.

When the three were finally seated on the train, they found there was plenty of room. Although he was glad to be riding in the right direction, Hans was disgusted at the apparently unnecessary delay. *Did the officer at the Siberian camp arrange this?* he wondered. He never knew the answer.

The three had not walked five miles until Otto gave up. He could no longer keep his balance from weakness, even though Hans helped him by giving him his arm to cling to.

"I am only slowing your pace, and it's no use. I can't make it. You two go on. Maybe you will meet someone to come after me," Otto moaned as he sank down in a heap.

"We will rest awhile," Hans said, rubbing Otto's legs to stimulate circulation. "Maybe Fritz and I can carry you."

Hans knew he and Fritz were also getting faint from lack of food and could scarcely walk that far themselves, but how could they leave Otto behind?

"Put your arms around us now," Hans said kindly. "Fritz and I will carry most of your weight."

Otto obeyed, but shook his head sadly. "We can't make it. If you don't go on, we will all three perish. If you go on, maybe you will be able to reach the village, and they will come for me. I will stay right here, so you know where to find me."

Otto's voice was weak and pleading, and Hans realized this was the only thing to do, though it would be hard to leave Otto.

Hans and Fritz plodded on, stopping to rest often. But knowing that Otto was back there waiting, and that if they tarried it might be too late, they went as fast as they could. With Hans nearly dragging Fritz, they all but fell as they stumbled into the village.

Loving hands took them in. This happened to be a village where many Chinese lived. The kind women prepared food for the nearly-starved men. They wept at the haggard appearance of the men. Upon hearing the story of Otto, arrangements were made at once to go after him.

"Otto's mother lives near the village," a man told Hans. "I'm sure she would want to go along if she knew."

"Someone go for her at once," Hans cried. "She should know."

With tears streaming down her face, Otto's mother pleaded for Hans to accompany them, so they would be sure not to miss him. "You know the spot where you left him lie, and we do not," she said.

Hans felt much refreshed since eating of the bounty the Chinese women had placed before them. "I'll be glad to go back with you," he said. "Be sure to take food for Otto. He may not be able to endure even the wagon trip in his weak condition." But Hans would not have needed to worry about food. Otto's mother had already prepared some to take along.

Never did horses seem to travel at such a slow speed, though they were urged on as fast as was advisable to drive them. At last they came near the spot and Hans called to the driver to drive slower. For another few minutes the horses walked on while Hans and Otto's mother stood on the wagon, searching every inch of the area with their eyes.

Otto's mother was the first to see Otto's form lying in the grass. With a loud cry, she jumped off the wagon even before the horses stopped.

Hans watched the still form of Otto. Was he still alive? His mother bent low, weeping. "Otto, my Otto. What have they done to you?" She stroked the thin face.

Slowly, Otto's hand reached for his mother's hand, but dropped limply at his side. He sipped the warm soup his mother fed him. Soon a smile crossed his face, and he said, "Hi."

There were no dry eyes for those who witnessed the meeting of mother and son. The food as well as the love she showered on him soon revived Otto to the extent that he felt ready to be conveyed to the village.

"Don't worry, my Otto," his mother murmured, weeping to see her son's wasted form. "I will nourish you back to health." She smiled through her tears. "But now I must be careful not to feed you too much at a time."

Hans was glad to be able to leave Otto in the care of his mother, but now his thoughts turned to Netta. He was anxious to go on.

Nearing the place where he expected to find her, his heart had some misgivings. He had not heard from her for so long that he did not know what to expect.

Lenchen was playing outside the tent when Hans approached the camp. Seeing him walking toward her, she fled inside. "Mama," she said, "a man is—"

Netta moaned, not even turning her head.

At that moment Hans entered and sprang to her side. "What is wrong, Lenchen?" Hans asked, hugging his child to him.

"Papa, Papa," was all Lenchen could say as she clung to him.

"Hans," Netta whispered, trying to raise her head. But she dropped back on her bed, struggling for breath.

Hans was down on his knees, taking hold of the limp, feverish hand. "Oh, Netta," he said, drawing her hand to his lips. "You are sick."

"Yes," she answered with a moan, holding her side, as she gasped for breath. Hans looked questioningly at Mutti, who had been watching the scene with tear-dimmed eyes.

"She not only has blood poisoning, but has also developed pneumonia."

"Is there no doctor available?"

"We have tried to get one, but to no avail. However, you are a godsend. The harvest is over, and they will move us back to the village within the next few days. I could not move her by myself."

Hans sat with Netta that night, trying to relieve her where he could, but there was no medication, only water and rags, which he used to bathe her leg and body. "Oh, if there were only more nourishing food," he cried, "there might be some hope."

Hans picked up Netta and carried her to the waiting wagon. He was more grateful than ever for the food the Chinese women had given. Netta was not heavy, but it took all his energy to carry her.

The move caused her pain and discomfort. Hans thought the road was more bumpy than he remembered. He tried to shield her body from the jolts by holding her all the way.

Carrying Netta to the small home he had built, he laid her on the homemade ceramic stove. It was warm, and the wind had been chilly on the ride.

Hans busied himself to make Netta comfortable. He wanted to seek a doctor, now that they were back at the village for the winter. How thankful he was to be able to be there to help, at least for three months.

Hans did not have any more success with a doctor than Mutti had — only a promise to see Netta when he next came to the village. However, they heard of a friend in the village who knew how to treat blood poisoning. She offered to come see what she could do.

"Bathe it in cold water," she advised, getting the preparations ready at once. "Twenty-four hours a day," she told Hans. "There might be a chance, but it is slim. You must be very persistent."

Mutti and Hans took turns soaking Netta's foot and leg in cold packs. Some improvement began to be noticeable, and Hans applied himself to do all he could to help the leg, sometimes lightly massaging it. This caused some discomfort, but afterwards actually relieved pain. Even the pneumonia improved. Still Netta was in a serious condition, and Hans hoped for the doctor every day.

Hans had gone to the canals to bring more water. The day was bleak, and a cold wind was blowing. *How glad I am to be here to do this,* he mused to himself. *If Mutti had all this water to lug, I'm afraid she would skimp on Netta's soaking. I'm certain this is helping.* Hans bent his head low against the cold wind and did not see the officer until he spoke.

"Are you Hans Reimer?" he asked with authority in his gruff voice.

"Yes, sir," Hans answered truthfully, not liking the ugly glint that was so evident in the officer's eyes.

Taking a paper from his pocket, he waved it in front of Hans.

"You are under a charge by the government for violating rules of the Communist Party. I have come to take you in for a hearing."

Hans was so shaky he could hardly keep his filled water buckets from splashing. "There must be some mistake." Hans tried to keep from shouting. "I have been on furlough only about twenty-seven days, and I have a written permit for a three-month leave."

"This is a new offense," the officer stated with a steel-like firmness that sent chills down Hans's back.

"Besides, my wife is sick with blood poisoning which she received when she worked for the government. Now she has also developed pneumonia. I am badly needed to help, for we have not been able to receive any medical help."

"You will be permitted to carry the water home and tell her good-bye," the officer said, his voice rising. "But make it snappy, or . . ."

Hans knew it was useless to say more. The officer was there to apply the cuffs as soon as he set the water down.

"Oh, Hans," was all Netta said when she saw the officer. But tears flowed down her cheeks and down Mutti and Lenchen's as well.

"May God care for you," Hans called as the officer led him away.

Hans's trial was short. Someone had given his name as an offender in order to receive an added bread allotment.

He was sent to a concentration camp even farther north than before. Temperatures fell as low as ninety below. However, the atmosphere was not as damp. Still, as Hans walked to work, his frozen clothes rattled upon him.

Here, too, men died like flies from malnutrition and severe temperatures.

Walking to one of the outbuildings one evening, Hans was suddenly confronted by two men. Hans did not like the looks of them. He had heard about other men who had been caught, had had their clothes stolen, and then had been abandoned to freeze.

Hans knew he was trapped. He stopped, taking one step to the side of the fence. At the same time he stepped on something hard. Reaching down he picked up an iron bar that had been lying there. The two men were hunched, ready to spring on him, when Hans lifted the iron rod. They stopped short.

At that moment, Hans remembered Mumsy's words. They were almost as audible as if she had said them just now. "Never return evil for evil." Hans pitched the rod across the fence, as far as he could throw it. Straightening himself to his full height, he calmly asked, "What do you want?"

Almost as if Hans had thrown the rod at them, the two turned and vanished behind the buildings. Hans never saw them again.

Hans was shaken. God had intervened by his mother's teachings. God still cared. Hans's inner being cried for more knowledge of a God who could keep two evil beings from doing him harm. He wanted to serve God, but how?

Hans had been transferred to Barracks No. 10. A few older men were mixed with the group that was huddled around the stove that evening. Hans felt sorry for these elderly men on starvation row. He knew it must be very hard for an older person to do such strenuous work in such cold temperatures.

Hans drew near the warmth of the stove. Most of the men were new to him.

"Brother Manisky, continue with the Bible verses, please," one of the men requested.

Hans listened with interest, his eyes focusing on the elderly man who began to quote from the Bible.

"Let not your heart be troubled: ye believe in God, believe also in me. In my Father's house are many mansions: if it were not so, I would have told you. I go to prepare a place for you. And if I go and prepare a place for you, I will come again, and receive you unto myself; that where I am, there ye may be also.

"You see, friends," the kind voice of the gentleman explained, searching the hungry faces around him, "I will soon be with Jesus, for He has promised to come for me. I will see those prepared mansions on high, where no hunger or offenses can enter. Also no evil. Whoever wants to may come, if he believes in Jesus as his Lord and Saviour. You see, Jesus paid the price for our redemption when He was nailed to the cross. He died in our stead for the remission of sins. Don't put it off, boys. Confess your sins. He is willing to forgive you. He even asked the Father to forgive the sin of those who nailed Him to the cross. For He said they did not know what they were doing."

Lovingly he looked at his listeners. "We, too, must pray for these men who mistreat us. And we must not feel bitter toward them. They also do not know what they are doing. They can kill the body, but they cannot harm the soul if we do not let them. Pity them. Think of their sad fate when Jesus comes to take us home and the day of judgment comes upon them."

The old man shook his head sadly. "Let us pray," he said, dropping his head into his worn, calloused hands.

All the men bowed their heads as he prayed. Hans had never heard anyone pray like this before. He even prayed that Stalin would be given wisdom and understanding to govern the country wisely, and that he might feel God's power and come to the knowledge of the truth. He prayed for the officers, that they might fulfill their duties in a godly, honest way, and that the prisoners might be given strength to endure the persecution they faced without retaliation. He asked the Lord to give all the people at camp a good night's rest and heal the sick. He prayed for the loved ones at home. Hans could feel the very presence of God in the room as the aged man prayed.

All the men added their *Amens* when he was finished.

Hans's head remained bowed for some moments, as he silently expressed his own deep longings. He sensed it was the leading of God that he had been transferred to this place where he could hear the Gospel message.

Most of the men shook hands with Hans, introducing themselves before the gong tolled, telling them to put the lights out and retire.

It was the same every night. The men gathered around the stove while the aged brother quoted verses from the Bible and explained the way of salvation. Hans knew he needed more understanding of the Bible truths to find the way of salvation. He did not yet know how to respond to God. However, he grasped all he could and pondered on the verses daily. He was especially helped by the prayers, sensing the Spirit's probing and hearing His call, waiting for a better understanding.

Hans was walking home from work. He was tired, hungry, cold, and rather discouraged. Thinking of Netta, he wondered if she had improved after he left. Or had she gotten worse when only Mutti was there to take care of her? He had written, but there had been no answer yet.

I am farther north, and it took some time to get my address in the file, Hans mused to himself, *but I should hear soon.*

His thoughts turned to meeting around the warm stove and listening to the kind brother's sermons. He must make it a point to talk personally to the brother, for he wanted that inner longing satisfied.

So deep was Hans in thought, that he did not notice he had turned onto the wrong path. Before he knew what was happening, two men had grabbed him.

They will rob me of my clothes and let me freeze, was Hans's immediate thought. Quick as a flash, he tore himself loose and dodged behind a bush. That was the last he remembered.

When he came to, he felt dazed and uncertain. Finally he decided he was riding in an army truck, heading for somewhere, but he didn't know where.

Chapter 17

RETURNING STRENGTH

Netta's life hung between life and death. Her temperature rose to frightening heights. Only through persistent cool compresses could Mutti bring it down. After Hans left, some of the women aided her at times, for which Mutti was thankful. Getting water from the canals, however, was up to her.

The scarcity of food was so pressing that Mutti's strength began to fail, making the care of Netta doubly hard. Besides trying to catch a hedgehog for soup, she needed to rise early and work late. She longed for spring when the mushrooms grew. Yet those had to be gathered, and with hundreds of others searching for food, she was not always successful. She had three mouths to feed.

Mutti had saved a supply of hulls which had been allotted to them. These contained fiber but were of little food value. But this is what she prepared for Netta when other methods failed. Opening a bag of soybean pods in an effort to make some soup, she longed for some fat to add to the tasteless pods.

"Don't you have a hedgehog to add to it?" Lenchen asked, her stomach aching for food.

"No, Lenchen. I have not been lucky enough to catch one this week yet. Your mama does need something more nourishing to get well."

"I'll see what I can find," Lenchen said with determination.

"Wait, I'll go with you. Since Mama is asleep, it will be okay."

Wrapping up against a cold wind with the rags they owned, the two went out to catch something to eat if possible.

Netta's sleep was actually a coma, from which Mutti feared each day she might never awake.

"Why are all those people running?" Lenchen asked.

"Looks like there might be some food somewhere. Let's follow and see."

Just outside the village there was indeed some food. A mule had died. The government had taken all of the carcass, but had left the stomach and intestines.

Mutti and Lenchen came up too late. The hungry mob was grabbing pieces of intestines. Mutti stood back and watched. She felt something under her foot, and looking down she saw the mule's tail lying in the weeds. Meanwhile, Lenchen drew near to the crowd. Seeing her chance, she dived between a woman's legs, and came back with a handful of greasy intestines.

The woman turned and called out angrily and would have chased Lenchen, but Lenchen was too quick. She dodged and ran to Mutti.

The two were pleased with their find. "This tail and the fat you got will indeed help to make a nourishing soup for Mama," Mutti told Lenchen.

"The woman would have liked to grab mine," Lenchen said thoughtfully. "But I wanted it to make Mama well."

"I think she had her share, if I noticed correctly, so don't worry, Lenchen."

"Let me bring in more sticks, Mutti, to cook the tail-bone."

"Yes, we need more. We will cook it with the hulls, and what a feast we will have!" Mutti said happily.

The pleasant aroma of the soup filled the one-room house.

Mutti patiently spooned the steaming soup into Netta's mouth. But Netta groaned and turned her head away. "I'm dying," she told Mutti between gasps of breath. "Don't write to Hans because I want him to come back for Lenchen."

Mutti bent low to catch the feeble words. "No, Netta. This nourishing soup will strengthen you."

Lenchen came, too, and tried to encourage Mama to eat.

And so they labored on with starvation at the door. Yet somehow when spring drew near, they were still living, and Netta was slowly improving.

The Russian women had more ration allotments than the German women, and sometimes they had a handout for Lenchen when she played with their children. Lenchen always brought a bit of it home for Mama. Many of the Russian women were kindhearted and sympathetic, but they had to be careful whom they helped, or they would be in trouble with the authorities.

One day Netta woke from a long nap. Mutti and Lenchen were off in search of mushrooms. The sun shone brightly, warming the house. Netta held up her head weakly, resting it on her elbow. She stretched her leg and winced at the pain, but it was not as sore as it had been. Should she? Could she? Netta pondered, struggling to get into a sitting position.

Her head throbbed, and she almost swooned with dizziness, but she clung to the edge of her bed to steady herself. Sliding toward the wall, Netta grabbed the edge of the table and pulled herself up. She stood a few moments, trying to gain her balance. How frightfully weak she was! Her knees almost buckled under her. But Netta did not give up. She wanted to feel the warmth of the sun and breathe the fresh air.

Shielding her bad leg as best she could, she inched toward the door and opened it wide. *Oh, how good the fresh air smells,* she thought, breathing deeply. Another step, and she was outside. Should she go back in? Suppose she fell and could not get back. But the sun was too inviting.

Edging along the wall, she reached the corner of the house. At the other end of the house she noticed a low spreading plant. Could she make it that far?

Inch by inch, Netta made her way forward, holding onto the outside wall for support.

Reaching the plant, Netta carefully stooped to pull it up. The roots held fast at first, not yielding to her feeble strength, but at last she held it in her hands. "Swine weed," she said. The plant looked good to her hungry eyes. The leaves and stems were firm and fleshy. Brushing the sand from the roots, Netta began to inch her way back again. Several times she stopped and leaned against the wall.

Back in the house, Netta rested, but not for long. She needed hot water to prepare the swine weed to eat. She could scarcely wait until it boiled. Pouring the hot water over the plant, she let it sit but a few minutes before she ate it, roots and all. "Delicious!" she said, licking the dish. Her stomach felt better than it had since she became sick.

Her thoughts went to Hans. She had not heard from him since he had been placed at the concentration camp in the Far North. Was he still alive? Her heart ached to think of the cold and suffering he had to endure. She could scarcely recall the time he was at home and his leaving.

Netta lay down and slept. It was a sleep of recovery. Thus, Mutti and Lenchen arrived home, finding her still asleep, or so they thought.

They had not found many mushrooms, for it was yet a little early in the season. But they had caught a hedgehog, which Mutti now skinned and made ready for the pot.

When Netta woke, she surprised Mutti by getting out of bed. Mutti was alarmed. She sprang to her side. "No, Netta! You will hurt your leg and make it worse."

Netta smiled. "No, Mutti. I was up and walked outside while you and Lenchen were gone. I found a swine weed growing behind the house. I steeped it in hot water and ate it. It gave me new strength. Somehow I believe

God let it grow there especially for me. What did you find
to eat?"

"Only two small mushrooms besides this hedgehog.
But we will have something to eat today at least. Lenchen
went in search of a few sticks to cook the dinner."

"I think I will be able to do some knitting now, Mutti.
And I think it is good for my leg to get some exercise. So I
plan to walk some every day. I will use this stick crutch for
awhile yet."

Mutti and Lenchen were overjoyed to have Netta up
part of the time. They still applied cold packs to Netta's leg,
but they were certain now that Netta was going to get well.

Netta still hoped for the doctor. She realized that her
lungs had not returned to normal since her sickness. But
still the doctor didn't come.

The garments which Netta knitted were sent to the city,
and Netta received bread for pay. When she and Mutti knitted for ten nights, they usually knitted enough garments to
receive ten small loaves of bread, which amounted to about
two pounds. The pay seemed small, yet it fed them enough
to keep them from starving.

Mutti also received a small allotment of bread for
hoeing in the government fields. She earned one hundred
grams of bread per day, scarcely enough to keep one
person alive. But it helped.

Netta's daily walk slowly but surely brought back her
strength. A few of the kind Russian women came to visit
and were glad to see her improving. The scarcity of food,
however, slowed her progress, and she remained weak.

"Come over here," one of the women called to her one day when she was out walking. "I want to see your knitting."

Netta picked up her knitting and went to show her neighbor her work. Once she was inside, out of the sight of watching eyes, the woman placed some cheese and bread before her and told her to eat while she looked at her work. Another time it was sweet pickles and tea with some bread. The added food helped Netta greatly, and she was deeply appreciative.

But in spite of continuing to gain in strength, Netta's leg was still very sore and discolored.

"How is your leg?" one of the Russian women asked her one day while she limped along on her walk.

Netta showed her the bad leg.

"Come inside and let me massage it," she told Netta.

Netta bit her lip to keep from screaming as the woman kneaded her leg as one would knead bread dough. "Always rub upwards," she told Netta, showing her how to do the massaging herself. "It will help to carry the infection back with the returning blood. Your body will better dispose of the infection that way."

Netta felt the improvement in her leg when the woman had finished with the massage. She thanked her kindly and promised to continue to massage it.

"I hope they will not ask me to work in the fields just yet," Netta told Mutti. "My leg is improving, but I'd hate to make it worse by overtaxing it."

However, the mayor of the village soon heard of Netta's improvement and sent an officer to visit her.

"We have a farm east of here where they need a book-keeper," the officer informed Netta. "It seems the past bookkeeper was not very efficient. Besides, the foreman did not get along with her. So we will come for you in two hours. Be ready."

Netta was pleased to think of earning more bread at a job she was trained for and which would not be too taxing for her leg.

Chapter 18

DEATH SENTENCE

When Hans was unloaded at a prison, he realized that guards had been responsible for the clubbing. *'Tis a wonder I came to at all,* Hans thought, feeling the size of the bump. *If it weren't for Netta and Lenchen, I almost wish I hadn't.*

The authorities let Hans know that he was under arrest. At first they gave no reason for it. However, after some counsel with the two police who had abducted him, they came up with the offense of loitering on the way home from work.

"Put him in Cell 0-2," the officer told the warden as he gave the handcuffed Hans over to his care. "We will bring you your sentence later, Reimer," he added, as Hans was led away.

Hans had slept but a few hours on the hard prison bed when he was roused from his sleep. He tried to collect his drowsy thoughts, hearing the rattle of the keys at his door. Two officers stepped inside.

"We have brought the verdict of your trial," one officer said, holding a paper in his hand. They offered no apology for waking him in the night.

"This is to verify," the officer read, "that Hans Reimer is sentenced to die. He will have seventy-two hours of grace to write to his family if he so desires."

Hans was startled at the severity of his sentence, but he only nodded his head. He was used to taking orders without retaliating.

Having done their duty, the two backed out of the tiny cell and closed the door. The key turned, and their heavy steps sounded down the hall outside.

Hans sat in deep thought. He had done nothing worthy of death. In fact, he had done nothing worthy of arrest. But here he was with a death sentence hanging over him.

Hans's thoughts went back to the kind brother who had taught them from the Bible. *Jesus was free from guilt too. He took my sins upon Himself and went to the cross. Even though He was not worthy of death, He did not resist the penalty they put upon Him. And He did it so that I might live.*

Tears of repentance flowed down his cheeks. *I will do as my Saviour and Lord did. I will not resist, and God will recompense.*

Hans's thoughts then went to Netta. If only he had a way of knowing whether she had recovered. There was small hope of receiving a letter from her at this address before they carried out the sentence.

Thus Hans's thoughts raced until around three o'clock in the morning when he was roused from his reverie by an officer opening his door again. "Follow me," the officer ordered.

They couldn't even wait until the time appointed, Hans thought as he followed the guard in silence. He would not have time to write Netta.

Without a word of explanation, the officer led Hans outside and placed him in a patrol truck.

Where to now? Hans wondered, but he did not ask. He resigned himself to the execution.

Still, Hans rode in suspense, not knowing exactly when or where he was to be executed. Finally they arrived at another prison. Here Hans was locked in a very small cell. A small stove took up much of the room. A narrow shelf, hooked to the wall, could be let down to serve as a bunk.

Here Hans sat and tried to write a few words to Netta. *But what shall I write? I guess I'll write the truth. If they do not want to send it, that's their choosing.*

My Dear Netta and Lenchen,

I have done nothing wrong, but I am condemned to die. I long to see you both again. Meet me in Heaven. If only I knew you were well and had food and clothing, it would be easier to die. Teach Lenchen, and find a church.

I have only love for you, and for our persecutors, too, as Jesus did. I am not afraid to die for I am not guilty.

Good-bye, my love, good-bye, dear Lenchen.

Papa

Inwardly, Hans grieved for Netta and Lenchen. "I must die and will never see their dear faces anymore," he groaned audibly. "They need me to provide and care for them."

Hans longed for the old brother to explain more of the way of salvation from the Bible. He tried to recall the Scripture verses he had heard. They seemed so distant. He groped for them, but they slipped farther away from his disrupted thoughts.

"O, Netta, my beloved!" Hans groaned again from the depths of his heavy heart.

Hans sat up straight. Had someone spoken? He was certain he heard a voice. Hans heard the voice again. "Pray," it said.

Hans looked around his cell. He even looked up at the ceiling. There was no one there. Surely God had sent an angel to tell him to pray. *So God knows, and He cares.*

Hans wondered what he should pray. He didn't really know how. Remembering the prayer Mumsy had taught them, he knelt behind the stove, which he felt was the only place where he would not be visible from the door.

"Our Father which art in Heaven," Hans began slowly and reverently. "Hallowed be thy name. Thy kingdom come. Thy will be done in earth, as it is in Heaven." Hans prayed on as Mumsy had taught him and ended with, "Amen! Amen!"

He knew as he prayed, "forgive us our debts, as we forgive our debtors," that he had forgiven and that he had received forgiveness. His heart became light. The former depression and heaviness were gone.

Hans prepared for bed. He thanked God for all that had taken place, knowing God was able to keep that which he had committed unto Him.

Hans went to sleep almost immediately. He slept like a baby all night. A great peace enveloped him such as he had not experienced before. The sweetness of it filled his entire being.

Chapter 19

WOLVES

Netta arrived at the farm with mixed feelings. The home they had left behind, though bare, was still home. She was more skeptical yet when she saw the disorderly farm. Poor management was evident everywhere. But Netta also knew she had no choice. Like slaves, they were placed wherever they were needed.

Netta was still more disgusted when she saw the disorder of the books and found that the mayor of the village and the foreman went on frequent drinking sprees. In fact, the foreman was in a drunken stupor most of the time. Small wonder the farm was so neglected!

Netta had been especially glad for the bookkeeping job because of her health. Just before they had left, the doctor had finally examined Netta's lungs. "The infection is gone," he told Netta, shaking his head, "but there is a dark spot on the left lung about the size of a cup which really is a hole left in the lungs from the extensive infection with no medication.

"You are lucky to be here," he added, dismissing her.

Netta had hoped that Mutti could do knitting here also, for it had helped keep them from starving. But there did not seem to be any opportunity in this place. Also, there were no kind neighbors to give any handouts, and Mutti and Netta found it hard to keep alive.

Netta longed for a more intelligent foreman who would manage the farm wisely. When the farm did not produce to the government's expectations, the food was all taken. Yet she knew that with the mayor and the foreman both drunk, they could not expect any improvement.

What a curse drink is, Netta thought. *It not only wastes their goods, but brings much unhappiness and hunger to others.*

She had to wonder why the government put up with slothful, drunken foremen, yet mistreated faithful workers.

Since Netta's bookkeeping job did not bring in enough bread for them, Mutti needed to work in the fields, much to Netta's dismay. Though Mutti was willing to work for more bread, there still was not enough to give her the strength she needed to do her job. The food became less and worse as time went on.

An aged couple working on the farm died from starvation, and Netta wondered if they might be next. *They have no heart,* Netta thought. *Perhaps this is their way of getting rid of us Germans.*

Netta, however, was persistent in her bookkeeping. Though it took much effort and time to untangle and straighten the records, she ended up with an excellent job.

The mayor from the village checked her work, and finding the books in good order, approached her about teaching school.

"Our regular teacher resigned, and we are needing one. I think you will be able to manage okay. Report for work at school Monday morning."

Netta again had no choice, but had to take whatever was assigned to her. Would she be able to walk the distance? Her clothes hung loosely from her shoulders. Her body had been shrinking considerably. They were always hungry. The herbs and roots Mutti brought in did not satisfy a starving body. She seldom brought in a hedgehog, for the surrounding country appeared to be overly hunted for wildlife.

When the school term ended, Netta was moved to another farm to do bookkeeping there. She was pleased with this move, for here the foreman did not drink and managed the farm wisely. He kept a cow, and each worker was allotted a liter of milk a day. He gave Netta an extra liter for Lenchen.

Here they prospered and gained in health and weight. The workers were given a half acre of garden where they could raise food.

They also were given potatoes to eat and flour to make bread. Yet Netta would not waste any food, nor let her family eat excessively.

"We need to take care of food wisely," she told them, "for if we do, no one will need to starve."

There were five families living on the farm, so they had to share the garden with the five. But Netta considered it a great privilege.

Mutti showed Lenchen how to plant the seeds and hoe in the garden. It was not always easy but they were greatly rewarded when the pumpkins were harvested in fall. They were so large that they had to be rolled in. Mutti also picked five pails of beans and harvested five carts of potatoes from their plot.

Lenchen was overjoyed. "We need not go hungry now," she laughed, sitting atop a huge pumpkin. "With these sweet pumpkins and all these potatoes, maybe we can share with someone who is hungry."

Netta had not heard from Hans for a year, not since she was moved to the new bookkeeping work. Did he yet live? She had written when they moved. Had he not received it?

She longed to hear even if it was a message that he had died. Living in this suspense was difficult. Still, she did not give up hope. Lenchen spoke less of Papa's absence, and Netta wondered if she would know him if she saw him.

"They are going to move us again," Netta reported to Mutti when she came in from the fields. "Another book-keeping job to straighten out."

Mutti's face darkened. "I had hoped we would be able to stay longer, now that we have found a place where we have enough to eat."

"I did too, Mutti. But you know we cannot choose. Perhaps this will be a good place too. At least we have gained back our weight in the year we lived here. We can be thankful for that."

Though Netta tried to encourage Mutti, she herself felt doubtful, knowing there were few places they would be favored as they had been favored in the past year.

Netta was indeed disappointed at the new job. Here, too, drinking and neglect were evident, not only in the bookkeeping, but in the farm and village too. Why did there seem to be plenty of drink while food was almost too scarce to find?

After the books were untangled and set in order, it was winter. Again they lost considerable weight and knew not how they could survive the cold winter months with no additional food rations.

One day the mayor came from the village to examine the books. Finding them in good order, he said, "You are to accompany the foreman to Lemintal to see that these books arrive safely there. We have been asked to bring them in before the middle of November. So if there is anything you want to do with these records before handing them over to the higher authorities, I recommend you do so at once. However, I find nothing amiss in them."

Netta had the books ready. She borrowed fur robes and prepared to dress warmly, for it was cold, and the ground was covered with snow. They would travel the twenty miles or more by horse and sled.

The foreman was so drunk Netta could scarcely make him understand about the trip. What could she do? Would he be able to guide them through the wilderness?

Netta thought of the wolves, which were usually hungry in the wilderness this time of the year. She knew they were dangerous when they were half starved. She would need a goat-hair rope to tie to their sled to keep the wolves away.

Netta hunted for a rope among the neighbors but found none. However, the foreman had one hanging in the shed.

"Be sure to bring the rope," said Netta, pointing to the hairy rope. "The wolves are likely to be on a rampage these days."

The foreman assured her he would bring the rope, and Netta hoped he would stay sober enough to know what he was doing.

"Be ready by four," he said. "It will be a long day to cover thirty miles by night."

Netta hoped it was not that far, but she knew they needed to start early. Taking her share of milk, she heated it to give to the foreman in case he was too drunk by morning. "It will help sober him up a bit," she told Mutti.

"Take my milk for yourself then," Mutti offered. "You will need it for the trip." Netta refused, saying she would make out. Secretly she hoped the foreman would see that she received some lunch on the way and also when they reached Lemintal.

The foreman helped tuck Netta in with the fur robe, then covered himself with another. "Ready," he called drunkenly, settling back against a pack on the sled. "Giddap."

Netta almost forgot. "Did you bring the rope?" she called, bending forward from the backseat.

"Naw, 'tis all right," the foreman spluttered, slapping the reins against the horse's flank.

"Whoa!" cried Netta. Crawling out of her furry covers, she grabbed the reins, bringing the horse to a halt. She was not going without the rope.

The foreman seemed not to notice. Netta sprang out of the sled and ran into the shed. The moon was shining, and she remembered somewhat where the rope had hung. Yanking it off the hook, she tied it around her waist. "I'm going to take care of this," she muttered, wrapping herself into the fur covers again.

Reaching forward, she punched the foreman. "Ready. Let's go."

Netta was glad for a cold wind, for it helped to bring the foreman out of his drunken sleep. She had the warm milk wrapped and against the hot soapstones by her feet. If necessary, she would give him some later. What Netta did not realize was that the foreman had taken plenty of alcohol with him. In fact, he was hardly in a responsible condition most of the way.

Through the moonlit night they rode in silence, the runners of the sled squeaking as they sped over the frozen snow. Netta tried to speak at times to rouse the foreman into wakefulness. For more than an hour they made good time. *The horse seems to know the way,* Netta mused, but then she realized there was only one marked road through this part of the wilderness.

Netta dreaded to see the moon slip behind the horizon. But even then, the bright stars on the white snow gave them some light.

Another thirty minutes went by. The horse slackened his speed at times, then broke into a run again. Before long morning light would appear in the east.

"Wolves!" the foreman shrieked, seemingly fully awake now. "I left that rope at home." He reached for the long whip in the socket.

Netta had heard their whining yelps in the distance too, but now they were coming nearer. They were on their trail without mistake.

Unwrapping the rope from her waist, she tied it securely to the post at the back of the sled. "I have the rope," she called. "It is dragging behind us on the snow."

"That is fine, but I wish I had one to tie to the horse too."

In spite of the rope dragging behind them, Netta felt chills go up and down her spine at the sound of the bloodcurdling howls. She could see a large pack of wolves advancing rapidly behind them. They would soon be near the rope. Would it stop them? What would keep them from an attack from the side, or front? If the wolves attacked the horse, they would be goners.

If one attacks us, the whole gang will dive in to tear us apart, she reasoned fearfully.

The wolves stopped, close. Then with a loud attacking yelp, they raced for the sled.

One large wolf was in the lead. Netta thought he was near enough that one large leap would bring him to the sled, when suddenly his nose almost touched the goat-hair rope. He let out a howl that echoed into the night. But he did not come closer.

The whole pack crowded in but would not advance closer than the end of the rope. Several wolves slithered into some bushes and came out near the horse. The foreman's whip lashed at the wolf.

With a howl that sent fearful echoes ringing over the hills, the wolf dropped back. Another tried it too, coming in from the side. Again the foreman's whip snaked out, driving the starved creature off. For more than a mile, the wolves followed in an effort to get some food, but without success.

Netta watched them slacken their speed while the foreman tried to get the horse to pick up speed. One by one, the wolves dropped back.

Even as Netta watched with relief as they slunk off into the darkness, she could not help but pity the hungry creatures. *They are as thin as we are,* she thought. *Perhaps even more so.* How well she knew the feel of an empty stomach!

Netta was greatly relieved when at last she was safely home again. The foreman was more drunk on the homeward way than he had been when they went. She hung the goat-hair rope where she had found it, thankful she had not forgotten it, for it certainly had saved their lives.

"A letter from Hans," Mutti cried, as soon as Netta reached home.

Netta looked at the postmark and noticed the address was not the same. She carefully opened the letter and found that he had written from prison.

Tears flowed down her thin cheeks. "Hans is in prison," she said sadly. "They have marked out most of his writing, so I have no way of knowing why, or what has happened to him."

Netta now remembered to remove the stamp. "Yes, there is an X marked here," she stated with a faraway look. "He is in trouble or perhaps even dead by now."

Netta grieved for Hans. The letter had been written at least a month before.

Chapter 20

RELEASE

————

Tonight is the night, Hans told himself. *It is now seventy-two hours since they read my death sentence. They always work their evil doings at night,* he thought. *Maybe they think no one will find out about it.*

Hans went to bed and slept well all night. No one came to carry out the execution.

Perhaps the guards overslept or were drunken last night. They will not likely forget tonight, Hans decided.

Again Hans slept through the night undisturbed. He wished they would not prolong the time. *It is just more suspense and stress for my starving body.*

Night after night, Hans thought they would come to take him. Yet a week elapsed, and he was still occupying his little cell.

The eighth night he was awakened by two officers. Hans noticed that one of them had a pad and pencil. *At last,* he thought, for he had long ago resigned himself to die. He rose from his bunk, ready to follow them.

"Sit down," one of the officers ordered. "We have something to ask of you."

Giving Hans the pad of paper and a pencil, he commanded, "Write."

Hans looked at the officer in surprise. "Write? What do you want me to write?"

"Write that you want mercy! A chance to save your life."

Hans was quick to see into their tricky schemes. They had no evidence of anything that would condemn him, but if he pleaded for pardon, they would have evidence that he was guilty.

"I will not ask for mercy," Hans stated flatly. "I am not guilty. However, I am already condemned to die. It is to be fulfilled, is it not?"

"You can write something," the officer insisted, not accepting the pad Hans tried to hand back. "Perhaps they will give you freedom, or give you a release."

"No, I will write nothing," Hans said firmly. "I need no pardon, for I am not guilty." Handing the tablet back, he looked the officers squarely in the eyes and said in a calm, firm voice, "I have nothing to ask of you."

The officers left. It was three o'clock in the morning.

The next night the officers entered his cell again. "Are you ready?" they asked, waking Hans.

Hans rose from his bunk. "Yes, I am always ready. My clothes and boots I keep on, and all I need is my heavy, quilted outdoor coat."

As he followed the officers down the dark hall, his thoughts were drawn to Netta. They would send her a notice of his death, but they would hardly tell her they had executed him without a cause. He felt calm in his soul.

But instead of leading Hans outside, they put him into another cell. Two other men awaiting execution were kept in this cell.

Hans realized that this was death row. The execution would shortly take place. Still, a week passed and Hans was still waiting.

"They try to keep us in suspense to destroy our sanity," Hans told the other two, who were deeply depressed. Hans tried to cheer them by telling them of the verses he learned from the Bible when he was still at the camp in Siberia. He tried to explain what he knew about salvation.

One night Hans's two companions were taken. He never saw them again. He presumed they were executed.

A month rolled by, and still Hans was kept in the cell on death row.

Several months later, Hans was roused from his sleep one night at one o'clock. He followed the guard outside to a waiting truck. From there he was taken to the train station. Others were being transferred also, and guards kept careful watch over them.

On the train, Hans was placed in the criminal coach. The train guard was told to keep him under special guard. Hans inwardly smiled at the implication that he was too dangerous to be left unguarded.

Entering the coach, Hans looked around to find a seat. The men stared fearfully. Hans realized that while he was in prison, he had had neither haircut nor a shave. His hair was long and his face hairy. This, plus his starved condition, no doubt gave him a wild look.

But fear rose in his own heart at the rough-looking bunch before him. He was classed as one of them. Yet he shrank from the thought of close contact with them, for he heard their vulgar language.

Turning to find a seat at the other end of the coach, Hans saw two rough-looking fellows coming at him. Murder seemed to glow from their wicked eyes.

"Don't come near me!" Hans cried, clenching his fists. "I can lay you down cold!"

The two stopped short, turned, and went back to their seats. No one else tried to molest Hans the rest of his train ride.

Inwardly Hans began to question what he had done. *They took me for a murderer like themselves,* he reasoned. *Had I let them come on, there may have been greater trouble, perhaps even a riot.* But deep down he knew what he had done had risen from fear, not love. And he felt remorse.

Hans was now placed in the worst-classed prison in the country. Here were dangerous men, murderers, and the insane. But somehow Hans found the favor of an old, rough character on the same ward. This man warned the others to leave the "aged gentleman" alone, saying, "If any of you touch him, you will be done for."

Hans didn't understand why the man protected him.

But he learned that the others respected this man's fists, and none went against his orders.

For five years Hans worked hard labor in this prison-concentration camp. Though others were taken and their sentences were carried out, Hans did not receive a call. He no longer lived in suspense, yet he knew his time might come any moment.

Coming home from work one day, Hans walked slowly to his cell, which he shared with four others. His thoughts were drawn to Netta and Lenchen. He had written since arriving at this camp and had heard from Netta, but there had been an X under her stamp, so Hans knew she was either not well or was in trouble. It weighed heavily upon his heart.

"Wait," an officer called, walking toward him. "Tomorrow you will be a free man!"

Hans did not appreciate mockery.

"Free? Please, sir, don't mock me." Hans turned to walk away.

But the officer insisted. "Yes, tomorrow you will be a free man."

Hans faced the officer. Tears wet his eyes. Could it possibly be true? He had served only half of a ten-year sentence, and besides, he still had a death sentence hanging over him.

He had been away from home now for fourteen years, and this seemed to be the general way of life. But a faint hope began to dawn in his heart.

The next day Hans learned that Joseph Stalin had died. The concentration camp workers would be freed.

Freedom, however, was not "on the morrow." There was a lot of red tape to go through before Hans's release could be verified. In the process, Hans was taken to still another prison.

Here Hans was more privileged in that he could visit with the other prisoners.

After a few weeks, he learned to appreciate visiting with a young man in another cell on the same floor as he.

Hans soon learned that the young man was acquainted with the Bible. Furthermore, the boy's father was a Christian and sometimes came to visit his son. Hans enjoyed their fellowship.

"I still have hopes of finding my wife and daughter," he said with tears. "But whether I find them or not, I want to find a church that teaches and practices the truth of the Bible. I had a pious mother, and I want to meet her in Heaven.

"She taught me right from wrong when I was but a lad," he explained, "and it has helped me more than I can tell. I was only twelve when she died. The revolution had just begun."

"Yes, we all have gone through trying times, and we hope things may change," Hans's friend replied. "But if the Communist Party continues to rule our country, we may never see freedom here. I would advise you, when you get out of here and find your family, to move to Frunze. You will find it a peaceable area, and you will find Christians there too."

Hans thanked his newfound friend, saying he hoped they might meet again.

In the next two and a half months, Hans was transferred to two more prisons before he was finally released, a free man.

Walking through the prison doors for the last time, Hans wanted to shout, "Free! Free!" But though he was now free to go to Netta, getting there was another problem. He had no money and nothing to eat. He would have to try to catch a ride with someone in the free world who was traveling south.

Chapter 21

HOME AGAIN

---

*N*etta was moved from farm to farm to straighten books that were out of order. Most of the time they were placed where little food was to be had. But occasionally, they would find a place where they fared somewhat better. In the fifteen years she worked at bookkeeping, she was placed on eighteen different farms.

When the war ended, things began to improve slightly, but not until Stalin died did Netta begin to receive money for her work.

Netta was very economical and began to find ways of making some extra money. She then found and rented a piece of land large enough for keeping a few goats and raising a garden. There was even enough pastureland for her to grow some hay for the goats.

Lenchen was overjoyed when Mama brought home the first nanny goat, and her joy knew no bounds when the goat presented them with twins.

"They are so cute, Mama," Lenchen exclaimed, hugging them. "I want to help take care of them and learn to milk Nanny."

"You may help feed the kids and Nanny, but right now we need the milk and so do the kids, so we will wait awhile to teach you how to milk her. You may learn later, perhaps when the kids are old enough to milk."

Netta prospered under careful management. Mutti helped with the work at home so Netta could work away.

Netta tried to save every penny. "When Papa comes home, we want to be ready to go where he wants to go and have something to start with," she told Mutti and Lenchen. She had received the letter that he was to be released, but she was not certain just when it would be. He had mentioned he was still being transferred from place to place. He also wrote, "The food is still bad. I am looking forward to more nourishing food when I come."

And so Netta watched and waited, every morning thinking that might be the day. But another month passed, and Netta was still waiting.

One beautiful morning, Netta was working in the garden, hoeing the weeds and sowing a few more seeds. Lenchen helped her, as she loved to work outdoors, especially in the garden and with the goats.

"The kids are growing too big and getting into mischief," Netta exclaimed as they chased them out of the garden. "We must sell the billy kid. That would help some at least."

Lenchen didn't like the thought of parting with him, but Mutti explained that they had the nannies and that Lenchen must be content.

Lenchen had learned to milk Nanny and often cared for the goats without Netta's help. So when Netta sold the billy kid, she gave Lenchen a little of the money. "It is time she learns how to save money and how to spend it wisely," she told Mutti.

Netta arranged knitting for Mutti so she would have something to do, yet wouldn't do the heavier outside work on the farm. "But it is not good for me to remain indoors all the time," Mutti objected. "I want to keep up my strength. And it is a pleasure to work when one has proper food to eat."

"That's true, Mutti," Netta said with feeling, "but I do want to care for you because you had to work so hard to help take care of us once."

And so a few more weeks went by. One evening, Mutti told Lenchen, "The sun is low in the west. I think it's time to milk Bonnie." They had sold the goats after Bonnie, a Jersey cow Netta had bought as a heifer, had her first calf.

Lenchen took the milk pail and went outside. A neighbor girl had come to watch Lenchen milk Bonnie. She also liked to help Lenchen feed the other animals they had collected on the farm.

"I'll throw some hay down for Bonnie before I milk," Lenchen called to her friend, climbing to the hayloft in the open shed.

Netta had stepped outside and was admiring the sunset. The flaming red and rose colors reached across the sky, touching the soft clouds overhead with a splash of delicate pink.

Netta's thoughts turned again to Hans. Was he about to be released? Could it be possible that they would still make him serve the other five years?

She heard a truck come up the village street. It slowed to a stop in front of the house.

Netta saw a man on the back of the truck. Could that be Hans? How old and thin the man looked . . . not like Hans. Slowly and with effort, the man climbed from the truck and with faltering steps walked toward her.

It was Hans! "Lenchen!" Netta called. "Papa is here!" She ran to help him, for he was almost too weak to walk.

Lenchen had just pitched some hay down for Bonnie. Like a flash she slid down the hay and ran to meet Papa.

Mother and daughter met him at the same moment. With tears streaming down their faces, they all but carried Hans to the house.

Hans was so weak that he almost collapsed. They put him on a chair and pulled him to the table. "Quick, Lenchen, bring a bowl of the milk I heated for soup."

Netta fed spoonfuls of milk into Hans's mouth. "Just sip a little of this until you revive a bit," she encouraged him.

Lenchen held Hans up with her embraces. Her tears mingled with his as she kissed his thin cheeks. "Oh, Papa," was all she could say. How poor and thin he looked! She had suffered from starvation too, and could very well sympathize.

The warm milk soon revived Hans, so that he could speak. "My dear Netta, this is the best-tasting milk I ever had. Where did it come from?"

Lenchen hugged him. "We have a cow, Papa. She gives us lots of milk and butter."

Hans could hardly believe they owned such riches. "Oh, if I could but give a cup of this milk to my friend still at the prison."

Hans took the spoon now and fed himself. Netta pulled up a chair and sat down beside him, tears still flowing from her eyes. She wept not only from the sad condition Hans was in, but from the joy of having him back again. She was so thankful he had not died.

"The cow, Netta. How did you get her?"

Lenchen laid her cheek against Papa's head. "Papa, God provided for us, so that you would have milk when you came home."

Hans was glad to hear Lenchen speak with such faith. *Netta has taught her about God,* he thought.

"We had goats first," Netta explained, "but they increased so fast and did not stay within our bounds, so they had to go. Then I bought a cow."

"Yes, Papa, the nannies had triplets and twins, and soon we had seventeen. They were so cute and playful I didn't want to sell them, but Bonnie's calf is cute too."

"Lenchen thought God gave the increase of the goats as He did for Jacob," Netta explained. "She thought we should not sell them, but the neighbors did not appreciate them when we could not keep them at home.

"But we are relating too much for Papa in his weakened condition," she continued. "We must let him go to bed and rest. Tomorrow he may hear more.

"Please, Hans, do not eat too much at one time," she worried. "I will bring you more to eat later."

"Let's thank God." Hans bowed his head. With tears of appreciation, Hans thanked God for His deliverance, for life, and for the food He so abundantly provided. He thanked the Lord for keeping their family during the trying times and for bringing them together again. He asked God to supply the needs of those still in prison and to give them a quick release.

Netta put Hans to bed, and he slept almost immediately.

Hans was much refreshed the next morning and was not as tottery.

"Food does wonders to gain back your strength," he said, giving Lenchen a hug. "My little girl, how you did grow!

"Now Netta, will you tell me how you came to live on this nice farm?"

"You see, I continued to work at the bookkeeping job after the war, and I saved what I could. It was by God's goodness that we found this little farm to rent. Now we sell some milk and the extra vegetables we can raise. Also, Mutti's knitting helps. We could not lay away much at a time, but with consistent effort, we have accumulated enough to get ahead a bit."

"We have ducks and chickens too, and have some eggs to sell and even some meat." Lenchen's enthusiasm bubbled over. "I just love this little farm, and we need not go hungry now."

Hans smiled. "Your mama managed very well, and I hope before too long we may be able to move to Frunze."

"Why move, Papa?" Lenchen said in dismay. "This is such a nice place to live!"

Lenchen was tired of moving and leaving everything behind. Often they had had hard times after a move.

Hans related how he was advised to move to Frunze to find Christian friends who believed the Bible and lived it.

"I think Papa is too tired to hear more tonight," Netta said, noticing weariness creeping over him.

After giving Hans a supper of hot milk soup and cooked potatoes, Netta suggested that Hans retire, even though he had rested most of the day.

"Now that Papa is here, if he is not too tired, maybe he wants to read us a chapter from the New Testament." Netta smiled, handing Hans the book.

Hans received the book with astonishment. "Where . . . where did you find this?" he asked, looking at Netta as if she had stolen it.

Netta smiled at his surprised stare. "A Russian woman who used to call me to her house to look at my knitting often gave me food. One day she gave me this spiritual food. It being a German Testament, she could not read it, and she knew I could. She was such a kind lady."

Netta's eyes were wet with tears as she remembered her kind friend. "If it had not been for thoughtful friends and kind hearts, I don't think we would have pulled through," Netta explained.

"I know, Netta. So many people died here and also in the camps and prisons. I was even sentenced to die, but God saw fit to bring us together again. Why, we do not know, but we need to serve Him the rest of our lives for His keeping and protection."

Hans handled the precious book with care. He did not as yet know the books in the New Testament, nor just what he should read. But the Bible fell open at John 4.

He read about the woman of Samaria and about Jesus resting at the well. It was an interesting story, but his thoughts were almost too weary to grasp the meaning. Reading on, he came to verse 21, where Jesus said to the woman, "Woman, believe me, the hour cometh, when ye shall neither in this mountain, nor yet at Jerusalem, worship the Father. . . . God is a Spirit: and they that worship him must worship him in spirit and in truth."

Tears slid down Hans's cheeks, as he meditated on the Scripture he had just read. His thoughts turned to his own mumsy when she had tried to teach him. He had lost much time in teaching Lenchen, but he hoped it was not too late. He realized that the seed of faith was already sown within her tender heart. Now it needed to be nourished with the Word of God. He knew he needed to study the Word more, in order to teach her its truths.

Hans closed the book, then sat awhile with closed eyes. Netta and Lenchen waited in silence, knowing he was thinking deeply.

"Let us pray," Hans said, dropping to his knees.

Hans again thanked God for His kind leading and protection while they were parted and for bringing them together again. "Dear Lord, You know that we do not understand Thy Word as we should. Help us to find true Christian friends and a church where we may learn more of Thee.

"Help us, Lord, and direct our ways. We wait on Thee. Amen."

Netta helped Hans up from his knees and led him to bed. "It is too good to be true," he whispered to Netta. "It is even good to be pampered and loved again," he said smiling, as he pressed her hand to his lips when she pulled a quilt up over him.

"Good night, dear," she said. "Rest well."

Lenchen was up early to do the chores. She wanted to be finished before Papa got up, hoping he would be strong enough to walk outside to see the animals and the farm.

Mutti was preparing breakfast, not wishing to disturb Hans and Netta, though she heard them talking in their bedroom. There was so much to relate and talk about.

"When the war was over, we were permitted to have Sundays off," Netta was saying. "Not at harvesttime but in the winter. Then we *Frauen* started to meet Sundays to sing hymns and to read from the New Testament. We did not have anyone to explain it to us, but it was good to get together and encourage one another in our trying times.

"Lenchen soon learned verses by heart, and her soul seemed to receive nourishment from them as a body does

from food. Already she is a faithful believer, and under-
stands the Scriptures better than I do, Hans.

"Lenchen also writes nice poetry and is a willing
helper. She enjoys children and likes to read some of the
stories to them from the Testament."

"I noticed she is getting to be quite a lady," Hans admitted. "With such desirable talents, some boy will be looking
her way before too many years are past. I am not ready for
that yet. I have lost too many years of her life. Now I want
to make up for some of them."

Netta laughed a low chuckle. "Yes, I have seen boys
notice already."

"Huh," Hans said with disgust. "Lenchen is too level-
headed to accept boys' attentions yet."

"That may be true, Hans, but some of these boys have
a strange religion. The Mongolians and Afghanistans think
if they can catch a girl, or steal her, she becomes his bride.
We have some very nice-looking boys around with that
religion. They are good boys too and real gentlemen."

"We will see to that," Hans grunted.

"I smell Mutti's breakfast. Perhaps we should get up.
She is keeping it warm for us, no doubt," Netta said, helping Hans rise.

"I am already much stronger," Hans said cheerfully. "I
think I can manage by myself now."

Lenchen could hardly wait to show Papa around. He
had to see Bonnie first.

"I bought her as a heifer," Netta said. "Now she has a
calf and gives us rich milk. She is paying for herself already.

The chickens and ducks we started from eggs the first year. Now they lay eggs both to eat and to hatch too. Our feathered flock is increasing each year."

"Are you strong enough to walk out to the vegetable garden, Papa?" Lenchen wanted to show him the nice vegetables growing there.

"I think so, if I take my time. You and Mama have done a very fine job, handling this farm without a man."

"The men on the other farms sometimes hindered us," Lenchen said, guiding Papa to the garden while she tried to steady him.

Hans looked at Netta for explanation.

"Irrigation," she said. "In the daytime, they opened the gates to let the water from the canals into their fields. But this shut off the water to mine. I had to fix the gates at night to irrigate my fields and garden, often around one o'clock."

"You really have a nice little farm here, Netta, but I have decided the Lord did not spare us to enjoy the things of this life but to labor for Him. I think we should make plans to move to Frunze."

"You must be stronger before we can think of moving; however, we can work to that end."

Hans enjoyed the warmth of the sunshine. Even the air was better than he was accustomed to breathing in prison. All was in his favor to gain back his health.

"You have not told me if the doctor ever came to see you when you were so sick with the bad leg," Hans remembered as they slowly walked back to the house.

"Oh, he came to see me after they learned I was better. It was just before I left for the bookkeeping job. I was quite well again. He did x-ray my lungs and said I have a hole in my left lung about the size of a teacup."

"What!" Hans exclaimed with alarm.

"It was well I had bookkeeping to do, even though the foremen tried my patience with their drinking. I doubt that I would have pulled through if I had had to work in the fields like the other German women."

"That's true," Hans said seriously. "Many didn't make it."

"It was a sad time," Netta admitted. "It was so hard on Mutti when my sister Mahalia died. Mutti thought she should have died instead of her daughter."

"It is a miracle Mutti is still here, at her age," Hans said, shaking his head. "But I am glad she was here to help when you were sick," he added with feeling. "Did she have to work hard?"

"Yes, Hans, the government did not care about age. She had to work with the rest of the women in the hayfields, or on the threshing crews—all the heavy work that men do. I guess they thought they would work and starve the men to death in the camps and the women on the farms. The women also dug canals. And the drinking of the guards and foremen caused them to be terribly hard to please. It made them heartless." Netta sighed.

"There was much carousing among the officers at the camps too," Hans said. "It made the men beastly and cruel. But let us not dwell on those things or hold any grudge against them, for they, as Jesus' tormentors, did not know what they were doing. Oh, how rewarding it was to hear the precious words of life from the Christian brother in that cold North Siberian camp. It made all the suffering we went through worth it."

"I was often discouraged, Hans. I know I did not love our enemies as I should have, but I asked God to forgive me. Then I tried not to care or feel bad when we were mistreated, but it still hurt.

"Sometimes I thought that Christ would return soon. I wanted to be ready to go with Him. I just could not imagine things going better again.

"Let's see," Netta continued, "the years of '41 through '45 were the worst for us. After that, things went a little better."

"I see you have some brush cut and piled for fuel," Hans said. "Where did you get that? Who cut it for you?"

Lenchen arrived just then with a glass of milk for Hans. "Drink this, Papa. It will help you get strong." She laughed, squeezing his arm.

"Mutti and I cut it," Netta answered his question. "We borrowed oxen to haul it home. In the winter we had to go every ten days to cut more, for it burns so quickly. But it keeps us warm. The tiny pieces I twisted together to make them last longer."

"Was it far to go?"

"Yes, very far to travel in winter. So many people needed fuel that the nearest places were all cut before I could get mine cut."

"Whatever happened to Botkin—you know, the man who betrayed me for the promise of more bread?"

"Poor man, he never received any bread. His two daughters ate the bread, and he starved to death. The daughters, too, turned out to be bad girls. Their end was violent and terrible while flirting with some drunken officers."

"That's too bad. But the Lord will recompense. I knew Botkin as a friend and felt sorry that he should betray someone. I am so glad that I can say I never betrayed anyone, even if they tortured me and nearly starved me to try and get me to do so."

Hans and Netta prayed daily for the Lord's leading and direction. They were making preparation to move but did not know when would be the best time of the year to go.

Then, too, their family life had taken such a pleasant turn that none of them really were in a hurry to tear up and leave. They hated to do anything that might disrupt the joy they were experiencing since they were reunited.

However, they decided to leave it up to the Lord. He would give them a signal if they completely committed their lives to Him. And so they trusted, knowing He would not mislead them.

Chapter 22

MOVING

"*F*rau Mottli is intending to visit someone farther north tomorrow, and Mutti wants to go along to fish in the ponds. They also plan to stop on the way home to cut some brush. Lenchen has asked if she might accompany them. What do you think?" Netta asked Hans. She was glad he could help make decisions now.

"Will they return the same day, or is it too far?"

"Yes, they plan to return by tomorrow evening. I thought it would be a nice day off for Lenchen because she works so faithfully without complaint."

"If you are willing to spare her, I see no reason why she could not go, since Mutti will be along. Maybe she can catch some fish too."

"They will be taking the slow oxen and must leave early if they want to bring home some brush."

Hans was watching for the ox cart by early evening. He missed Lenchen's company, her happy chatter, and her soft, tinkling chuckles. "Should they not be here by now?" he asked Netta.

"No, it usually was late by the time we returned with brush, and we did not take time to fish or visit," Netta replied.

Hans waited outside until he heard the creaking of the cart wheels and the blunt stomping of the oxen. Then he went to meet Lenchen.

Lenchen slid from the cart, ran to Hans, and clung to his arm as if some danger were upon her. He could feel her shaking.

"Why, Lenchen, what is wrong? You are trembling all over."

"Take me inside, Papa," was all she would say, still clinging to him.

Hans placed Lenchen on a chair. "Now tell me, dear Lenchen, what has scared you or hurt you?"

Lenchen burst into tears, her pale cheeks turning to crimson. "He almost caught me," she sobbed brokenly.

"Who? Who almost caught you?" Hans was greatly disturbed now.

"Franz Hinti. I knew he liked me," she said, hiding her face inside her elbow. "I liked him too, but I was careful not to encourage him because he is not a Christian. I . . . I had hoped he would become one."

Lenchen sobbed softly, hiding her face in shame. Drawing a deep breath, she continued, "He is such a nice, pleasant boy, but he almost had me."

"Tell me about it," Hans encouraged, knowing Lenchen would feel better to get it off her chest.

"I have tried to avoid him for some time, but I should have told you." Lenchen shook with sobs again.

"I still do not quite understand, Lenchen. Did he hurt you?"

"Not physically, Papa, but if he had caught me, I would have been bound for life. Either I would have been his wife or would have faced death for refusing, and I cannot be the wife of a non-Christian.

"I was helping load the brush and was only a short distance from Mutti when he suddenly appeared. I ran like a frightened deer, reaching Mutti and the cart just in time. He almost caught my dress. Then he would have quickly dragged me into hiding!"

"Now we have our signal," Hans told Netta. "We must move as soon as possible and in the meantime keep Lenchen safely hid."

"Did he not say anything?" Mutti asked, trembling as badly as Lenchen.

"Yes, he laughed and called back to me, 'Not this time, Lenchen. The next time I will not be too late.'"

The Reimers sold their animals without any trouble. "God is blessing our efforts," Hans said. "I have hired a truck to move us. We want to leave in a quiet way. The less commotion among our neighbors, the better."

For three days the truck moved eastward before reaching Frunze. The Reimers were still in the southern part of Russia. Hans located a small house where they could live for awhile.

They soon found Christians, who readily welcomed them, so that when they attended church the first Sunday, they did not feel like strangers.

What a satisfying joy Hans and Netta found in fellowshiping with other Christians. Though the church had no regular minister, one came every third Sunday to feed the flock worshiping at Frunze.

The Reimers walked to church reverently. They could hardly contain themselves, knowing the minister was to be there. "You know," said Hans, "it has been thirty years since we have heard the Word of God preached."

"I suppose so," Netta answered with folded hands. "I am looking forward to hearing a sermon."

Lenchen had never heard a sermon preached, but she already enjoyed the youth group of that area. "They are so different from those back home," she told Netta. "Here the group's activities are Christlike."

All three of the Reimers sat with rapt attention as the minister expounded the Scriptures. They tried to absorb every word as it flowed from the minister's lips.

Hans visited with the minister later and expressed his sincere thanks for the message. "I wish you could be here every Sunday, but with so few ministers around, we do not want to be greedy. Others must hear the good news too.

"We have been without the Bible and without any Christian meetings. We are still like babies, but we are trying to learn what the Word of God expects from us. We do not understand all its teachings," Hans stated humbly.

"When people feel their weakness and their needs, they have come down the right path. Keep on learning, for we cannot understand it all in one day," the minister advised Hans.

Before the minister left, he called the group together. "I realize it has been years since we had church where people were taught to believe on the Lord Jesus and be baptized for salvation. Now you are again privileged with that offer which the Lord Himself taught when He was on this earth. This summer we hope to give instructions on the faith and have a baptismal meeting, so be prepared if you are interested."

Hans and Netta applied themselves to studying the Word of God from their New Testament. Some of it seemed confusing to them, and they wished for someone to explain it. "We need to know," Hans said seriously, "not just half of the truth, but all the Lord expects of us."

"It is hard to grasp some things, 'tis true, but Lenchen does not seem to be troubled about it," Netta replied. "She just trusts and believes what the Bible says is true. She plans to join the baptismal group for instruction."

Hans found work with a painter. And with steady work, he and Netta decided to look for a home that they might buy. "Our rent payments could just as well be payments on a house," Hans told Netta. "Don't you agree?"

"Yes, the rent comes due every month. Then the money is gone, and we are still just renting."

Mutti learned that her brother's widow lived at Frunze. Her brother had been taken and had never returned.

Netta's cousin Esta lived with her widowed mother, so Netta took time to visit her one day.

Netta and Esta were very happy to meet each other, for since the revolution, the finding of a relative was a rare experience. Their conversation soon turned to the Scriptures.

Netta explained that Hans and she were having some problems understanding some parts of the Bible. "Hans says we want to be certain we are doing the right thing and understand the plan of salvation. We find it hard to know how to receive it for ourselves. Lenchen does not seem to have any problem. She says she trusts the Lord and believes what His Word says. She has already accepted Jesus as her Saviour and is now getting ready to be baptized."

"I can understand that, Netta. She accepts Jesus and the truths of the Bible with simple faith, even as a child would. You are older and have been through trying times. You have taught yourself not to trust anything unless you know for certain it is right. I have a commentary you may borrow if you wish. It makes the Scriptures more plain, or at least it helped me."

Netta took the book home and read in it, comparing it with the Scriptures.

"It may confuse you more," Hans warned her.

"Suppose Lenchen and I read it and compare it with the Scriptures. If we find it unsound or confusing, we will stop reading it."

Lenchen now worked in the vineyards, adding her wages to Papa's. The savings for buying a house grew steadily.

"She works in the Lord's vineyard too," Netta told Hans, "for she now teaches a girls' class in the youth Bible study and a children's class in Sunday school."

Lenchen was nearing her nineteenth birthday when Herbert came into her life. Hans and Netta were well pleased with her choice. He was a fine Christian boy and was to be baptized the same time as Lenchen.

As time went on, Herbert became a frequent visitor at the Reimer home. Friends of Herbert and Lenchen began to assume they were betrothed, but Herbert had not actually proposed as yet. He was governed by an unusual prudence.

Herbert and Lenchen both enjoyed nature and liked to take walks when the weather permitted. These were times of expressing their deepest thoughts, and almost invariably they spoke of their love for the Lord. This was the oneness they shared.

True to Esta's thinking, the book she shared with Netta brought to light many truths Netta had not understood before. Though Lenchen had accepted these truths earlier, she found her faith being strengthened. As mother and daughter learned together, the tie between them grew ever stronger.

The truth finally dawned on Netta that the sacrifice of the Lord Jesus on the cross was made for her personal salvation. She also saw the sinful state she was in without receiving salvation for herself. And she realized she had not surrendered her all to the Lord that He might use her in whatever way He desired.

Hans and Netta both had a problem understanding the tribulation the Bible spoke about. Would it be before or after the rapture?

The book dealt somewhat with this, but Netta saw that the most important thing was to have faith and accept the salvation which Jesus offered them. "It is a gift of grace," she said to Lenchen.

"Lenchen, dear," Netta said humbly with tears of repentance. "I now see that the sincere believers are the only ones who will meet the Lord in the air when He comes to receive His bride. I want to commit my all to Him now. Will you pray with me?"

Together they knelt. Both prayed as Netta gave her life to the One who was willing to give His life that all might receive life eternal.

Rising from their knees, mother and daughter embraced each other. "Lenchen, I now know that all my sins are forgiven. How good it is to know I have that new life in Christ Jesus. It is too wonderful for words."

"I am so happy, Mama, to know how happy you feel. For I have experienced too, what joy it is to know the Lord as Saviour and friend. We are never alone when He lives within.

"And now, Mama dear, perhaps we can be baptized together. Wouldn't that be wonderful? We are already baptized with the Holy Spirit, but we need to be baptized with water as a public confession of faith."

And so, Netta entered the instruction class in preparation for baptism. Hans wanted a little more time to get some things cleared up in his mind. Being a deep-thinking man, he did not feel quite ready for baptism.

A large group awaited the day when the minister would come to perform the baptism ceremony. They sent him word that the applicants were ready. "If we tarry now," a brother stated, "who knows but that someone will be called from this life before he receives baptism."

The minister's sermon was about baptism. "We have that promise that he who believes and is baptized will be saved," he said, looking over the large group of applicants.

"The eunuch confessed that he believed Jesus was the Son of God, and Philip said he could be baptized on this confession if he believed with all his heart.

"Today that confession is just as necessary as it was then. There should be evidence in our lives that we believe from the heart, for the fruit of the Spirit is love, joy, peace, longsuffering, gentleness, goodness, faith, meekness, temperance, and against such there is no law."

Upon their knees, the applicants made their confession that they believed in Jesus Christ as the Son of God. Forty-four applicants were baptized into church membership that day.

Lenchen kissed her mother. "Now my joy is full. I thought maybe you would also be one of us today."

"I was ready, Lenchen, but since Papa was not quite ready yet, I thought it would encourage him if I waited for him."

"I am so happy for you and Papa. You will not have long to wait, for many others have asked to be baptized with the next class."

"Where was Herbert, Lenchen? I thought he wanted to be baptized today too."

"He had planned to be here," Lenchen explained. "But something came up that he was detained. The minister said he could be with the next group of applicants. Herbert sent his regrets and wants to come next weekend now."

Herbert did come to spend the weekend with the Reimers. It was springtime, and the weather was beautiful.

"It seems like a long time since I saw you, Lenchen," he said. "Especially did I want to come last Sunday to be baptized, but it was impossible."

"I was sorry too, but the week did not seem so long. My joy is full, and I have my Lord to speak to. I also knew you would be here this weekend, so I had that to look forward to."

"I am glad you are prone to look at the bright side of life, Lenchen. Why don't we go for a walk? The day is beautiful, and the leaves are pushing out fast with this warm sun coaxing them. I have no doubt but that the early spring flowers are blooming."

"I'll be happy to go, Herbert. In fact, I was about to mention it. The out-of-doors in spring reminds me of the resurrection of Jesus from the dead. It also makes me think of the time when our bodies will be resurrected, and we will go to be with Him."

"Well, Lenchen, we are now near the time of the year when Jesus was crucified, giving His life so that we might be with Him in eternity. He was the only One found worthy. He was pure, holy, and without sin. Yet He took our sin upon Himself, died on the cross as a ransom for our sins, and reconciled us to the Father."

"How true, Herbert, and all because of His great love for us. Now He expects us to love Him with all our hearts, and not only Him, but also our brothers and sisters, and even our enemies."

"The wisdom of His love is too wonderful for mortals to grasp fully," Herbert answered, opening the gate across the lane that led to the woods.

For some time the two strolled down the lane, enjoying the beautiful sunshine, and each being blessed with the love that filled their innermost beings. Their love for each other overflowed from their love for their Lord.

Lenchen was so silent that Herbert glanced over. He saw that her young face was deep in thought.

"You know, Herbert," she said softly, "I am sometimes so overjoyed with the love of my Lord that I long to leave this body of clay and go to be with Him." Her eyes filled with tears.

Herbert drew near to Lenchen. Her expression some-what startled him, though he doubted not that she was ready to meet her Lord. "My dear Lenchen," he finally said with careful earnestness, "I pray the Lord may spare you for many years to come. You are too young for such thoughts."

"Life is good when you are young and happy." Lenchen smiled then. "But with the Lord there is perfect bliss. And the young can die too, as I witnessed often when we lived on the Steppes."

"Let's not dwell on those bad times, Lenchen. They are in the past."

Herbert longed to tell Lenchen of his love for her and to ask her to be his bride, but he had decided he would wait until he, too, was baptized. Surely she was aware that he loved her. Her comment about wanting to go to be with the Lord had somewhat unnerved him. *Oh, well,* he thought, *she is overwhelmed just now with the love of Christ because of being baptized so recently.* He dismissed the thought from his mind to enjoy the moments that they were together.

Lenchen had inherited her mother's beautiful voice and would often be singing hymns or humming tunes. Now as they reached the woods, Lenchen was humming. She bent to pick a wildflower, one of the many that grew like a carpet over the wooded grounds. The tiny leaves just coming on the trees filtered the sunlight and made jagged, shaded patterns over the blooming masses.

"They smell so sweet," Lenchen mused, holding the tiny blossom to her nose. She held it for Herbert to smell. "Who could not believe in God, Herbert, with all this evidence? Who but an all-wise Creator could make it all? If God made the earth so beautiful, how much more beautiful will Heaven be?"

Lenchen had walked a few steps ahead across the floral carpet of the woodland. Then she turned to face him. Herbert held his breath for a moment. Her striking beauty, framed in this lovely spot, was almost heavenly. Was she indeed too perfect to remain very long on earth?

Lenchen's white kerchief, which she wore for a covering, was pinned neatly around her hair. It had slipped a little to one side, letting a blond curl escape. Her neatly-fitted blue dress was of a simple design, the full skirt reaching nearly to her ankles. To Herbert, her modest dress enhanced the Christian virtues and beauty within which he so greatly admired.

"Shall we go back?" Herbert asked in a hushed voice.

"As you wish. I'm ready if you are," she answered, her warm smile lighting up her beaming face.

She cares, Herbert's heart sang as the two walked back. *It shines from her eyes with the beauty and clarity of a rainbow. I hope she can read the love I have in my heart for her too. It won't be long, dear Lenchen,* he thought, *until I can offer you my heart in exchange for yours.*

"When will I see you again?" Herbert asked as they parted. "Will it be in a week, or sooner?"

"As the Lord wills," Lenchen whispered, looking deep into his eyes. "Let's leave it up to Him." She offered her hand in farewell.

Herbert touched her hand lightly. "I hope it will be sooner," he said softly, meeting her eyes. "It refreshes me to come, and your friendship means so much to me."

Lenchen watched the tall young man walk down the street with a buoyant step. *He's so handsome and good. What girl would not be happy to have a friend like him?* she pondered, thinking of the endearing things he had said during their walk. *But best of all, he loves my Lord. Without that I could not have a close friendship with him.*

Herbert had reached the corner. He turned and waved. Lenchen waved back. Her heart sang, *I hope too, he can come sooner.*

Chapter 23

DEATH

"I'll go to the well for water, Mama," Lenchen offered, picking up the pail. "After the storm last night, I'm certain the vineyards are drenched and too wet to work in."

"If you wish, you may, Lenchen. I suppose the earth is soaked far and wide this morning. It just poured rain, and with the wind, it sounded like a pretty bad storm. Please don't fill the pails too full, so they will not be too heavy for you."

"I am well and strong, Mama, and I feel so happy this morning, I think I could carry more than two pails of water." She laughed, running down the steps and out the gate.

Netta watched her for a moment and heard that she was singing. *That girl just bubbles over with joy since she was baptized ten days ago. I hope she may always rejoice in her Saviour's love as she does now. I am glad too, that she is not proud of her beauty. She seems to be entirely unaware of it. Beauty within, and beauty without,* Netta mused.

Netta returned to her laundering. While she rubbed the clothes and wrung them out, her thoughts went back to the Steppes. What a life would Lenchen have had if that boy had caught her? Lenchen would not have accepted him with his type of religion. He would have had the right, according to their thinking, to end her life had she refused.

Her mind drifted to Herbert. He and Lenchen were very much in love, she knew. *Soon Lenchen will be leaving her home to start one of her own,* she thought. But Netta was happy for her. *At least she need not wait ten years as Hans and I did.*

The door banged. *Lenchen back already? She must have hurried. No, it's Hans. Why —*

"What's wrong, Hans?" she asked as she went to meet him.

Hans's face was ashen and his voice was too choked to speak. Finally he managed, "Sit down, Netta." He pulled Netta down beside him. "It's Lenchen."

"Lenchen!" Netta cried. "Why she just left to bring water. I thought —"

A knock sounded at the door. Then the door opened, and Esta came in. "I am so sorry, Netta," Esta cried, tears streaming down her face. "They are bringing her now." Esta took Netta in her arms and wept.

Netta was weeping now too. The truth was evident. Something had happened to Lenchen, and she was dead!

"Tell me," Netta said, after she could compose herself. "Tell me what happened."

"The old oak tree at the corner blew over and fell against the high-voltage line." Hans tried to steady his voice enough to tell Netta. He held her close, and the two mingled their tears for a moment before he could go on.

"It broke the line, and charged the tree with electricity. Lenchen saw Joey running toward the tree as if he would climb it. Seeing danger she tried to keep him from touching the tree. She rescued Joey, but slipped, and her bucket hit the tree. It was instant death. She is with Jesus now."

"Oh, Lenchen, must we really part with you?" Netta wept as she gazed upon the still form friends had carried in. "We must let Herbert know at once." Netta realized it would be a sad blow to him also.

Herbert joined Hans and Netta in meeting friends before the funeral. Lenchen had endeared herself to all who knew her, and friends came from far and near to pay their last respects and to whisper words of comfort to the parents and to Herbert.

When Hans and Netta laid their only child into the grave, life suddenly seemed almost not worth living. Both Hans and Netta at that sad moment longed to lie there too, beside her.

Herbert remained with Hans and Netta a few days after the funeral. "You have been like a son to us, since you visited our home so frequently," Hans said. "I had hopes that someday we could claim you as our son, but now that Lenchen has been called home to live with the Lord, that cannot be. Yet we would be happy to have you come visit sometimes anyway. It will help us overcome this great sorrow."

Hans's kindness touched Herbert's grief-stricken heart. "I had the same hopes, Papa," Herbert said tearfully. "And since my papa does not live, I would be happy to call you by that name. May I?"

"I will be honored to be called Papa, for I will not hear that title from Lenchen's lips anymore."

Though Herbert and the Reimers mourned Lenchen's passing for awhile, they learned to resign this to the Lord also, knowing that she was ready and willing to be with her Lord and Saviour.

"She was baptized only ten days before her Lord called her," Netta would say. "She went to meet Him clothed in her spiritual wedding garments, still rejoicing in her first love."

Herbert shared with Lenchen's parents the conversation he had had with Lenchen the last time they were together. "She then expressed her desire to go to the Lord. It cut me to the heart at first. I had planned to wait until I was baptized to ask for her hand. Had it not been for that, I would have spoken that day. She looked so beautiful and pure to me." Herbert's voice broke, and he could not continue for some time.

"She also said we would leave it up to the Lord as to when we would meet again. I did not realize we would never meet again on this earth when I left her. She seemed to be so radiantly happy that day."

"We have plans to be baptized in two weeks when the minister plans to be here again. Will you be here then too?" Hans inquired.

"Yes, I want to join the group that will be baptized that day," Herbert answered. "The Lord willing," he added.

The church grew by bounds in spite of the strict government regulations which began to be enforced.

School-age children were not to attend religious services until they were eighteen. Neither were they to be baptized before then.

Hans was voted in as doorkeeper. In spite of the regulation, he opened the doors for the children. "We cannot turn them away," he said. "It would be sin. Jesus said we must become like a little child if we would enter the kingdom of Heaven. We need to teach them and bring them to the Lord, not turn them away from God and the church."

"You will be caught, Hans," a well-meaning brother told him one morning, as he let the children come into the church. "You had better obey the government."

"Ought we not to obey God rather than man?" Hans voiced his conviction without hesitation.

Thus the church became divided. One part yielded to the government regulations while the other part tried to obey God even if it meant persecution.

And so it was that the underground church took root and flourished. "The evil one steps in and tries to destroy that which is good," Hans told Netta sorrowfully. "Why must good friends and brethren be divided? Such confusion is not from the love of God, for our God is a God of order, not confusion."

Hans and some of the other brethren tried to heal the breach, but many insisted that the Word of God also taught them to obey the government. They were not willing to suffer more persecution and feared to go against the law.

"True, we need to respect our government and obey the law if it does not conflict with the Word of God," the staunch believers explained. "But we are willing to suffer for obeying the Bible truths. Too long we have negected our responsibilities."

It was a sad time for the brethren. Would the church fall apart just after having become reestablished?

When Hans, Netta, and Herbert were baptized, fifty-five applicants received water baptism upon the confession of their faith. They boldly stepped out to serve the Lord, regardless of what might come.

And so the church kept growing in spite of those who were faint and left to obey the government regulations. Every Sunday both old and young would stand and confess that they desired to be an applicant for baptism. Then they joined the class for instruction.

Hans, Netta, and Herbert were together talking one evening when Hans expressed himself about the wealth his father had had.

"I now realize how important it was to lose those earthly riches and even suffer persecution, as we did, so that we might find the riches of God's glory and the peace it has brought us. We now know that we are free from guilt, and by His grace we have the promise of eternal life."

"I know that I would not have been ready to die back then," Netta said quietly. "I am so grateful the Lord was gracious to me until I learned to know the way. I'm afraid if we would have inherited the riches your dad had, we would not have found the true riches in Christ Jesus."

"That is true, and now we know that these earthly riches have wings and fly away. But the riches we have found in our Saviour and Lord will endure forever, like the pearl of great price."

Herbert listened with interest. He appreciated Lenchen's parents and wanted to benefit from their experiences. "I am glad Lenchen didn't need to observe this schism in the church. It would have hurt her tender conscience, loving everyone as she did," Herbert said sadly. Tears wet his eyes at the thought of her.

"Yes, we too realize the Lord saved her from this world's suffering by taking her early," Hans said. "We know not what may follow if the government keeps getting stricter with the true Christians. It does not look very bright at times."

"It was very hard to give her up," Netta said tearfully, "but when I think of all the trials she need not face, and know she could go without pain or sickness, being in good health both physically and spiritually, I can actually thank the Lord for taking her home. He shared her with us this long. And she was a comfort to us, helping us to find the joy of the Christian life. She was a great blessing to us, a gift from God."

Chapter 24

GOOD-BYE

———

*H*ans brought the letter home and handed it to Netta. "It is from my sister Lenchen. She is still living and wants us to come to her in Germany!"

"Sister Lenchen!" Netta gasped. "I thought they had all died. Now . . ."

"Yes, she lives in West Germany. She must have managed to escape."

"And she says here," Netta read, "that she thought we were all dead. So far she has not been able to find any of the others."

"Sister has been working with the immigration department for some time, Netta, and has been helping people immigrate to Germany. She has been successful in getting some people out of Russia, but you need a close relative living in the country you're going to in order to get out."

Netta finished the letter and read it again. It was so good to hear from one of the family. They had thought no one else had survived. Laying the letter down, she asked Hans, "What do you think? Should we try it?"

"I have been thinking about it ever since I read the letter, and I thought since Mutti and Lenchen have passed on and since we have no close relatives, and . . . well, since the government is trying to persecute the Christians, perhaps we should at least try. What do you think?"

"I am ready if you are, Hans. We realize that persecution may be ahead, and we do not want to turn our backs now that we have accepted the Lord as our personal Saviour. Hans, I do not fear to die for my faith, but to think that you might be taken to Siberia or prison . . . well, I am just not ready for that again if we can avoid it. Since Lenchen lives in Germany, she, as a close relative, may be able to get us out of Russia. If we do not accept now, we may not have another chance."

"It would be wonderful to see a sister again." Hans's voice broke so that he could not speak right away. "Then to think that we may be able to find a peaceable church and that we could live without the dread of being torn apart again, I think it would be wise to see what Lenchen can do to get our immigration papers."

The Reimers soon had a second letter from Lenchen. She expressed her sympathy for the loss of their daughter, stating that she hadn't heard that they even had a daughter. She wrote, "Even though she isn't living anymore, I still feel honored that you named her after me.

"I have already started the ball rolling for your immigration, but have patience. It usually takes a long time to get everything set up. There is a lot of red tape to contend with.

"I have not been too well of late, but hope I will be able to get the papers through. I am like a child who can hardly wait for some good thing—I so long to see you again. That you may remain well until then is my prayer."

The letter encouraged them. They planned for a sudden departure in case the final papers should come sooner than they thought.

Their plans were kept a secret to all but a few close friends.

"We do not want to make any claims that are not certain," Hans said. "We never know how things might turn out, so we will wait to make it known to the church until we are certain."

Herbert was grieved to learn that Hans and Netta were planning to leave Russia. However, he rejoiced with them that they had found a sister living. "That would be good news," he said wistfully, "to learn that Mom or Dad would still be living. But I know for certain they died of starvation and hard labor."

Herbert then shared with the Reimers that he had met a girl whom he was seeing and he hoped they would not feel bad. "I know there will not be another Lenchen," he said. "But Maria is a nice Christian girl, and I feel the Lord has answered my prayer in finding another pure girl for me. I have been so lonesome since Lenchen died."

The Reimers were happy for Herbert. "We wish you could bring her sometime soon," Hans said. "We want to get to know her before we leave, and we do have some plans we would like to share with you two."

Maria found a warm spot in Hans and Netta's hearts. She would make a good wife for Herbert, whom they loved as their own son.

One day when Hans returned home from work, he found Netta sitting in a chair, her face tear-stained and pale. "Are you sick?" Hans asked with concern, as he walked to her.

Netta handed a written message to him, then whispered, "Sister Lenchen died."

Hans was shocked. He had so looked forward to spending some time with his sister; besides, they would need her in a strange land to get them started. "We might just as well give up going, I guess. I thought I was bringing good news for you, Netta. We received the immigration papers today."

The immigration papers to leave Russia and move to a free country! Netta sat up. "Hans, we still want to go, even if Lenchen will not be there to meet us and help us. She wrote earlier that there is a Christian church there and kind people who will be happy to help us. We will find friends."

"True, Netta, the papers are here, and the way is open. But I no longer desire to go, knowing we will not have a sister there now. Perhaps the Lord is not opening the way for us after all."

Netta rose from her chair and put her arm around Hans's shoulder.

"Hans! The Lord already opened the way. Can't you see? Remember, when you left prison, they still had you down for five more years. Do you have any assurance that they will not someday think it necessary to fulfill that sentence? No, Hans, the way is clear, and we want to go."

"I was not guilty to start with, Netta. Surely they would not say I have to serve the five years after they released me."

"No? Well, many things were not considered about whether the offender was guilty or not. They were still taken. Besides, did you forget your death sentence? Those things are kept on records. I will feel more secure in Germany than here."

Hans knew Netta was right. They did not know what would happen with the government still communistic. They certainly would not have another chance if they refused this one, for now they had no close relative outside of Russia.

"Will we find a church with sound teaching and principles? I think we could help here with the church. But perhaps . . ."

"We will trust the Lord, Hans. If He opened the way in these difficult times, He will also lead us over there. Do not fear, but trust."

And so, Hans and Netta decided to go. Since they could take nothing with them, they had already decided to leave all their earthly goods to Herbert and Maria, with the exception of a few items that they wanted to present to some close friends.

"Herbert has been so like a son and has respected us as his own parents," Hans told Netta. "They will need it too, because Herbert has very little money. Nor do Maria's parents have much to share. Or do you have a better plan?"

"No, Hans. I am happy to give them our house and little farm. We could not take anything with us if we died either. We can trust the Lord to supply what we need in Germany too."

Herbert and Maria set the date for their wedding earlier so Hans and Netta could attend it before they left for Germany.

They were very grateful for the Reimers' gift but expressed their unworthiness to receive it.

"We are happy to see you have it," Netta whispered to Maria, giving her a hug. "Then when we think back here, we will know that it is taken care of, and perhaps little children will be playing in the yard. You must write us often, for they will seem like our grandchildren, though we will never see them."

"Papa, I am sorry there is no way to repay your kindness," Herbert told Hans. "Maybe someday things will be different. How I wish we would be able to care for you when you need it in your golden days."

"Herbert, this is the third time we have had to leave all and move on. The Lord always provided in some miraculous way. We can trust Him for our future needs. When we leave Russia, we will never return. It is hard to leave so many dear friends behind, but we hope to make new friends in Germany. It should not be hard to find friends in a true church."

The Russian government had permitted the German people to have their separate meetings. And so, on a Tuesday evening, the evening of their normal Bible study, Hans and Netta met with the brothers and sisters for the last time. Hans was asked to give a farewell message.

Netta stood with Hans while he admonished the church to remain steadfast in the faith, regardless of what they might face in the future.

"Continue to teach your children, that the good seed may be planted into their tender hearts while they will readily receive it. For this is your future church. If you neglect your children, the church will have shipwreck, and faith will be lost. Then all is lost.

"Netta and I have experienced what a struggle it is to open our hearts to the Gospel truths after we were older. But our dear daughter Lenchen received the Word so readily in her youth.

"Reverence God and His Word at all times, for we receive not the crown at the beginning, nor in the middle, but only if we remain faithful to the end.

"We cannot expect to see your faces again," Hans said, weeping. The tears were also streaming down Netta's cheeks. "But may we meet in glory when we have finished our course, and the race is run.

"The crown of righteousness, that is laid up for us in that day, is not only for us, but for all those who love His appearing."

Hans and Netta dried their eyes and raised their hands in a farewell gesture. With smiling faces, they wished their friends God's blessings, receiving also best wishes and blessings from them.

And so, with renewed hope in their hearts and a strong faith in the Lord for the future, Hans and Netta turned their faces toward Germany.

Christian Light Publications, Inc., is a nonprofit, conservative Mennonite publishing company providing Christ-centered, Biblical literature including books, Gospel tracts, Sunday school materials, summer Bible school materials, and a full curriculum for Christian day schools and homeschools. Though produced primarily in English, some books, tracts, and school materials are also available in Spanish.

For more information about the ministry of CLP or its publications, or for spiritual help, please contact us at:

Christian Light Publications, Inc.
P. O. Box 1212
Harrisonburg, VA 22803-1212

Telephone—540-434-0768
Fax—540-433-8896
E-mail—info@clp.org
www.clp.org